Beneath
the Skin
of Sorrow

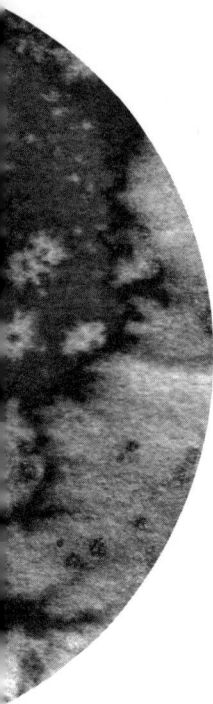

Bene
th
of So

NNENNA FREELON

ath

e Skin

rrow

IMPROVISATIONS

ON LOSS

Duke University Press   *Durham & London*   2025

Printed in the United States of America on acid-free paper ∞
Project Editor: Lisa Lawley
Designed by Courtney Leigh Richardson
Typeset in Garamond Premier Pro by Copperline Book Services

Library of Congress Cataloging-in-Publication Data
Names: Freelon, Nnenna, author.
Title: Beneath the skin of sorrow : improvisations on loss /
Nnenna Freelon.
Description: Durham : Duke University Press, 2025.
Identifiers: LCCN 2025001021 (print) | LCCN 2025001022 (ebook)
ISBN 9781478029113 (hardcover) ISBN 9781478061342 (ebook)
Subjects: LCSH: Freelon, Nnenna. | Grief. | LCGFT: Poetry. |
Prose poems. | Personal narratives. | Creative nonfiction. |
Autobiographies.
Classification: LCC PS3606.R44425 Z46 2025 (print) |
LCC PS3606.R44425 (ebook) | DDC 811/.6—dc23/eng/20250627
LC record available at https://lccn.loc.gov/2025001021
LC ebook record available at https://lccn.loc.gov/2025001022

COVER ART: Tissue ink mono/photoprint by Maya Freelon, 2025
(mayafreelon.com); starry background
courtesy Adobestock/jenteva.

INTERIOR ART: Maya Freelon, tissue paper and ink, 2005–2019;
author portrait courtesy Tanisha Walker.

Lyrics in "Widow Song," "Just You," and "These Stories
We Hold" reprinted with the permission of Chimusic
Co./ASCAP.

FOR PHIL   whose love still whispers   yes . . .

.

CONTENTS

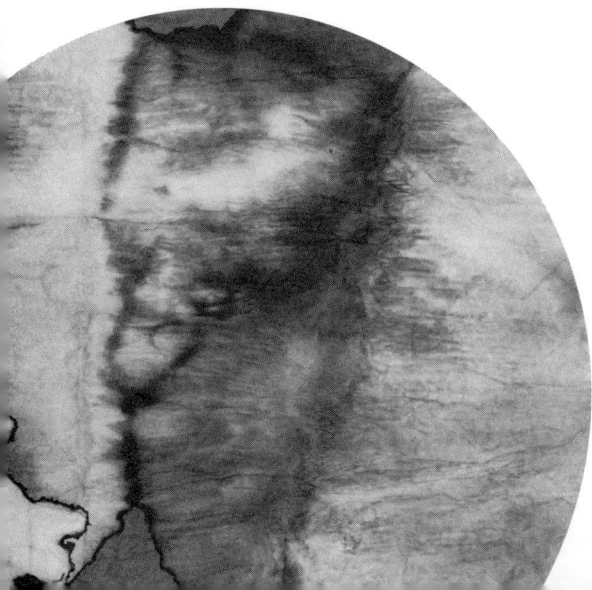

SECOND MOVEMENT
Stolen Moments

THIRD MOVEMENT

A Love Supreme

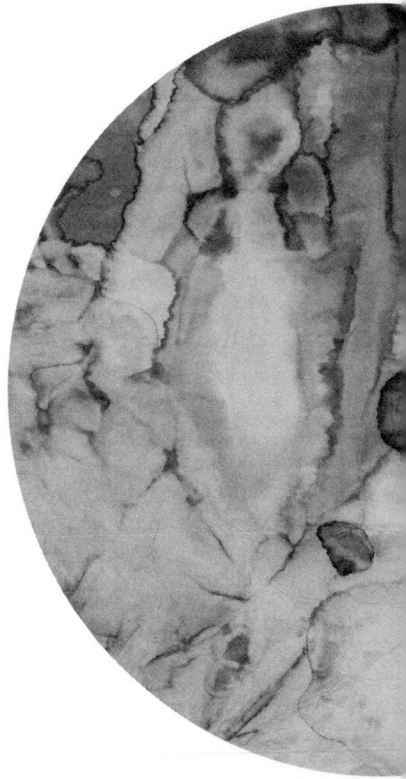

FOURTH MOVEMENT

Time Traveler

Coda

I had no idea the tools I learned as a jazz musician would become a lifeline in the sea of sorrow. My deep experience of loss led me to study an unfamiliar repertoire, to compose new melodies, to learn to sing in the dark, to swing in rhythm with sorrow's underlying pulse, and to find the notes of joy and hope in its cadence.

But mostly, I learned to listen patiently and more deeply than ever before.

I came to write this book by way of great grief. We'd been married nearly forty years when Phil, my beloved husband and soulmate, passed away from amyotrophic lateral sclerosis (ALS) in 2019. Six months later, my sister, running buddy, and best friend Debbie died from lung cancer. Compounding the absurd reality of these losses, Basie, my dog and sole remaining companion, died on August 9, 2019, one month to the day after Phil.

These layered losses were like a peeling away of self. Who am I now? A widow? A sister-in-loss? A singer with no song and no voice? Is there even a word for one who mourns the special kind of love that only a dog can offer? Those questions played on repeat, like a needle stumbling on an annoying scratch in an old soul record.

Gone was my joy and desire for life. I'd lost the ability to read or sing or improvise. The inner melody that had vibrated inside me since childhood went silent. My life broke into two parts: BP (Before Phil) and AP (After Phil). I struggled to make sense of these two eras. I was exhausted.

Jumbled phrases and bits of song tried to take form in my head, but I ignored them, assuming this was part of the grieving process. Yet the fragmented melodies and story remnants with their hidden messages wouldn't let me rest. They had stories to tell. Story fed song as song nourished story. And I listened. Intently. Deep listening allowed me to experience grief's resonance in places I didn't expect it. Slowly, in the months that followed, I began to gather pieces of a newly arranged self. And along the way, I regained pieces of my musical sensibility. It all felt strange, unfamiliar, and inharmonious. I had to sit with these feelings of discomfort as they began to perform, and to hear them with a spirit of curiosity and improvisation.

Since I was young, I'd always kept a diary. Writing was a way to keep counsel, to question, to create safety in the currency of words, but these musings—whether reckless, outrageous, or mundane—were private, meant for my eyes only. Thundering grief rolled through me, flattening everything in its path, my writing included. Swallowed whole, my entire life was sorrow-bent. I wrote to console myself, to find my way through the heartbreak. It didn't seem a path to rediscovery at first, but in time, writing gave rise to a new creative practice informed by, not in spite of, grief. Pushing against the visible weight of sorrow with words and whispered song allowed me to write and sing from a place made more precious by loss. I soon learned that my particular grief contained the universal. Everyone at some point experiences loss.

Beneath the Skin of Sorrow bears the sting of memory. It twists and turns through song and lays itself bare in the bones of prose, following the path of the awful ache and the awakening imagination of my broken heart.

The journey of grief is a unique process; I'm learning that creative paths are often overlooked when we think about engaging grief. This book called me to testify as Black woman, wife, widow, writer, singer, mother, grandmother, sojourner. I found that creative, improvisatory tools were the most authentic and sustainable for navigating the crosscurrents of my grief. I hope this book can help others find ways to swing with the unfamiliar rhythms of grief and to rest in between the pulses. One thing is certain: Your grief experience is your own; it belongs to you, and you cannot mess it up.

My mourning bowl was literally filled to the brim. It birthed my award-winning podcast *Great Grief*, as well as my album *Time Traveler* and a sixth Grammy nomination. In this book you'll read stories, essays, poetry, recipes, and lyrics colored by the beautiful and terrible tempo of grief. The musings in this collection are meant to be read in a manner that suits the reader. Nothing will be lost if you decide to flip to a page and experience a particular meditation, or story. These are refrains on the observable universe of grief. As such, they may be experienced as individual or sequential moments.

I approached this book as a composer might, by thinking about the collection as a large work in four movements. Although I've read about grief being described as unfolding in five stages, my musician's heart experiences it more as overlapping waves resonating in connection with something much bigger—something akin to love.

Grief is a mystery for sure, and each layer feels a certain way, holds some identifiable feeling like a key signature. Each of these pieces are revelations of my personal journey, evidence of having created some breathing space for my grief.

I grouped the musings together by their particular emotional heft rather than when they happened in the timeline. I borrowed the titles of well-loved jazz compositions in an attempt to reach for the feelings they contained. The four movements:

First Movement

"'Round Midnight" explores my arrival on grief's shores and my sudden realization of the shift from wife to widow. Here in the darkness of grief is where I first felt sorrow's wail rising in song and story.

Second Movement

"Stolen Moments" is a collection of musings on how grief reshaped my worldview. It's about looking at the world in the half-light of loss. Grief is a shapeshifter; the rules of time and space don't apply here. These reflections explore grief's resonance in extraordinary and mundane moments.

Third Movement

"A Love Supreme" contains meditations on joy and sorrow, the invocations of change, and the cadence of loss. The underscore of the past plays while the refrain of *what is* repeats. Reflected in our losses, there are treasures that grief can offer—if we can bear to look.

Fourth Movement

"Time Traveler" centers places of imagination and memory. These are new dreams and fictions and fables wrapped in personal experiences. Here, I write to affirm myself and find a way back to a sense of trust in the unfolding of life as it is now.

Some folks say grief is like a season, but that's not true. If it were, I could anticipate grief's end. I could look forward to the time when this emptiness will be over and done. What I've learned in my brokenness is this simple truth: The act of grieving is a living journey, one informed by love. By creatively engaging with your feelings and honoring sorrow, you acknowledge yourself as fully human. Doing so may allow you to become your own instrument of loving-kindness.

Believe me, I know that improvising may feel risky, navigating with no script or set of instructions. I've learned that hiding from or ignoring Grief encourages her taking up way too much space. We're building a new relationship with our grief every time we take even the tiniest step. I'm honored to have you take this walk with me. Let's begin.

RUBATO

Rubato in Italian literally means "robbed time."

In music, it denotes the freedom to freely interpret a particular musical phrase or passage. Grief altered the music of my life. It required that I *freely interpret* a new set of rules, sing in a new key signature. It was necessary to engage with this new tempo of grief even though there were times when it felt totally impossible to do so.

'Round
Midnight

'ROUND MIDNIGHT

Midnight sings the dark interval trembling between was and is.

The lyrics of the famous Thelonious Monk tune "'Round Midnight" report that things are pretty cool until the sun goes down. I'd have to agree. There's a kind of reckoning that begins when the sun slips beneath the horizon, trailing red and purple goodbyes.

That deep, dark midnight—the kind that most of the time won't let you rest—is what I'm talking about. When Billie Holiday sings "Good Morning Heartache," you can feel the slope of midnight in her voice, and somehow you know that come dawn, she'll be clutching at the serrated edges of sleep. This is the midnight that belongs in the script of every scary movie and is source material for all the ballads with sad lyrics.

There are other midnights, of course, the ones where you promised yourself to be in bed before today becomes tomorrow, or those where it's fabled that you'd turn into a pumpkin, but those aren't these at all. Grief introduced me to a persistent darkness, a midnight of the soul, one so deep it changed my relationship with myself and the world I knew.

For me, there'd been no inner morning's sunrise in the months since Phil died. I didn't realize it at first, but I'd been holding my breath, awaiting dawn's return. Daybreak was instead a sprawling darkness. I awakened incoherent, having slept or not, alongside reruns of the past. I mourned the loss of my husband and an inner *knowing* that I was also truly lost. How could one navigate the awful distances between *what is* and *what was*?

And all the while, the inner anthem played...trouble, trouble, trouble.

This particular midnight lay claim to all of me. My imagination sputtered and faltered in this dark thicket that I couldn't find my way through. It couldn't be wished or prayed away and, like smoke, seeped into every crevice and corner of my heart. The lyrics in the bridge of "'Round Midnight" speak of empty arms, and I understood the sentiment. Loss can drive you *out of your mind*.

I used to sing those words they lived inside a song.
Now they have become the land where I come from.

Wanting what cannot be *midnight*.
Turning back the hands of time *midnight*.
Sleepwalking in the shadows *midnight*.
All day and all night *midnight*.

This personal midnight became a kind of madness. Drop by drop, it rained darkness, and everything in my world was drenched. Was it depression? Maybe . . . probably. I felt estranged, as if I were gazing at a ghost who used to be me. Everything felt heavy—even breathing held a molasses thickness. My beating heart was an uneven staccato rhythm of fear.

I'd always thought of myself as a positive person—a thinker, a planner—but this midnight didn't allow for that and I didn't know how to function in this darkness. This was no place to find assurances or certainty. And that, of course, was what I wanted—encounters with the kind of knowledge that I was used to. A plus B and you arrive safely at C. Simple, right? Knowing, or believing that I knew, had served me well at other times. I'd been as certain of choices and outcomes as I was of gravity. But Grief changed all the rules, and now there was absolutely no reward for *knowing*, no gold star for the planner. In fact, this midnight offered no answers at all—right *or* wrong.

There was no room in my mind for a scenario in which Phil dies at sixty-seven years old; my baby sister, Debbie, dies at sixty-two; and I faced being truly alone for the first time in my adult life. What happened was *impossible* and forced me to let go of all my finely tuned plans. I didn't want to venture blindly in this wilderness of sorrow. I wanted the sweet song of life as it used to be.

Alone, disoriented, and facing the future with no sense of how I was going to survive was awful. I stiffened at the idea, certain there had to be ways *to think, to do* my way to safety. But there were none. And believe me, I really tried.

I struggled for a long time and eventually found the effort unsustainable; it was too much. I was grief sick—exhausted, physically and mentally. My heart was spent, leaving no choice but to give in to stillness. The *fear* of not knowing how life would unfold felt worse than the reality. Although my head was still full of argument, I began to quietly intone,

Let it be.

Something was whispering through my solitude, "It's okay, everything does not need *knowing*." And it was huge to accept this notion as gentle kindness, not a challenge. My learning to put aside the cumbersome apparatus of thought—

Let it be, let it be

—allowed quiet rest to arrive, slowing the tempo and permitting me to breathe in the grace of silence.

Releasing the *need to know* little by little, I stumbled across familiar feelings that at first I didn't quite recognize. I'd experienced them before, alongside creating, composing—singing on the breath—but way out here in this wilderness? I didn't immediately make the connection that deep mourning was calling me to a kind of improvisatory play. I was being invited to dance with my grief. Was this possible?

It seemed that my improviser's heart knew what my brain did not.

I became a believer in the dignity of self-tenderness, of being worthy and held in a loving embrace. I'd been hungry for answers:

Let it be scared of the unknown.

Let it be struggling in the darkness.

Let it be bone weary.

"*Let it be, child*" in a voice as warm as my grandmother's smile.

In the quietude, although these sensations were very faint at first, my eyes grew accustomed to not seeing, my heart and brain to not knowing. I could *feel* things spinning in the dark, thoughts and images sometimes just barely out of reach. I'd entered an altered state where all manner of glittering music and story—memories, dreams, letters, and recipes—were mingled in Grief's darkened crosscurrent. Some were beautifully composed shapes and others mere snippets of thought—flimsy notions not quite formed, on their way to becoming.

New forms of creative expression were forged in the fires of Grief; never in a million years would I have thought such a thing possible. Word spoken and word sung had always seemed to occupy different spheres, but Grief caused me to reconsider this notion. I found that by flowing between my voices, I could lean into what couldn't be fully expressed in either realm. I recalled the moaning and wailing women in church, these wordless expressions hip-deep in sorrow and consolation. And their wavering melodies destined for radiant wounded hearts.

The tools of creative curiosity seemed to belong exclusively to my other, happier life. Writing and singing from inside the cauldron of loss was not something I'd previously considered. But, inside this extraordinary darkness, my midnight heart sensed the familiar call-and-response of improvisation. Perhaps it was being *out of my mind* that loosed the knot at the throat of my heart.

In an over-thirty-year career, I've sung "'Round Midnight" on countless occasions. It's a song I loved singing. These days, I'm witnessing a strange confluence as "'Round Midnight" softly sings to my broken heart...

BEGINNER'S MADNESS

Phil died on July 9, 2019, at 7:02 a.m.

As Phil's final hour approached, we had taken turns holding his hands—those cool, slender fingers—and wiping his brow, celebrating his life as human, husband, brother, and dad. A playlist, one he'd curated, hummed in the background as we gently touched him. We shared lovely memories of hiking at the Eno River in North Carolina and the time he caught the big one on a fishing trip. Phil mouthed "I love you" once more, but soon he was silent as he drifted into that mysterious place adjacent to who knows where.

Our children (Deen, Maya, and Pierce) and Phil's sister, Randi, sat with him in our bedroom all night listening to his breathing, which began to change over the evening hours to a curious automatic breath. As we approached dawn, I had dozed into that sleep/not sleep mode when Pierce gently shook my arm. "Mom, I think he's gone." My first thought was: "Gone? Gone where?" I placed my head on Phil's chest, searching for his familiar heartbeat, but there was nothing. "What time is it?"

Pierce looked at the clock for confirmation. "7:02." I repeated those numbers, pondering their strange significance. Why not 7:03, or 6:45 for that matter? These numbers were our street address but more than that—they stood for our larger-than-life home where we had raised three kids, a dog, and a cat. Over the years, I'd often said to him, "Meet me at 702." Or if Phil asked, "Where are you?" I'd answer, "Oh, I'm at 702." Even after we'd downsized, the stories of our New Year's Eve parties at 702 were the stuff of legend. You had to be there. Pierce, our youngest son, thought the digits on the clock were a sign, some timing his father wanted us to notice.

So, at exactly 7:02 that morning, every atom within me thrummed change. And it was the day that I became quite decidedly mad. In that moment, lightning struck and I slipped out of phase with *normal* life. As the pinky-orange dawn gave way to the sunflower yellow of an early summer day, everything went dark for me. The sun brought no light at all. All of the spectrum of visible light fled in the face of Grief's twilight. Our bedroom was cloaked in darkness, and the lamp by the nightstand was powerless to change this.

But this was only beginner's madness. There was more swirling in the atmosphere, more strangeness to fumble through. I don't remember crying on that day. Maybe I did, but a grief-stricken memory is an unreliable tool for gathering facts. I recall rushing around the house, throwing away everything associated with being ill or dying.

"Sit down, Mom," our daughter Maya said. Confused, she watched as I was overtaken by the spirit of a frenzied clean-up woman. "What are you doing? This can wait."

I heard her words but couldn't stop myself.

Quickly, I tossed everything connected to sickness and death into two garbage bags and several donation boxes. I spun around the house, bent on the removal of all the tendrils of illness. During the days that followed, there was a color shift. The saturated hues from furniture, books, and artwork faded away, leaving only muted colors, a hint of what used to be. So, on top of going mad, was I also going color blind?

After that came the arrival of the tilt. The tilt was not only a personal unsteadiness where I was prone to lose my balance—tripping and falling over things seen and unseen—but somehow, everything *looked* tilted. Frames that housed paintings by Maya and Phil's masterful photography looked tilted. Why did every single frame on the wall seem to slope in one direction or another? I adjusted them one by one before grabbing the level from the garage. Surely that little bubble, perfectly balanced, would be an impartial judge of a right angle. I stepped back to look at my work, satisfied that I'd corrected a terrible wrong. But the next time I glanced at my handiwork the tilt had reoccurred. It was almost as if some invisible trickster was playing games with my mind, or else it was me, tilting toward insanity.

There were voices in my head and music that played, over and over, against the backdrop of the overwhelming quiet. These auditory hallucinations made it hard to think. Was my grieving brain trying to provide a bit of stimulation? It was pointless to use mourning sign-posts as a measuring stick for reality. And so, I decided that I was indeed mad. Embraced by the dark shoulders of sorrow, I was out of touch with the bones of this world. Maybe this would be a personal crazy, not the kind that would leave me disheveled, wandering the streets and muttering to myself. Does madness ease over time, lapse into a certain rhythm that you might grow accustomed to?

For some odd reason, Les McCann's version of "Compared to What" played on repeat in my head. McCann—no, the song—kept asking: "Trying to make it real? Compared to what?"

Am I trying to make it real? I wondered.

Phil knew all the words; well, most of them anyway. There's one line about tired old ladies kissing dogs that struck him as hilarious. He'd crack up every time he heard it. It would be just like my husband to send an inside joke in my direction from the other side.

"Oh, I get it now."

Phil was teasing me. He used to call me his old lady, but these days, I'm also the tired old lady in the song.

I laughed until I cried. That was funny, sort of, Phil. Very funny.

NOT DEATH

but dying.
Corridor tilting toward
a narrow passage
New limits
outer, inner
The subtle sway
of dust's return
Not death but dying.
An insistence upon fluency
In this strange dialect
Speaking without tongues
I ask, Who am I
once death carries me
in her wide mouth?
When I, swept clean
of name and place,
am settled on
that dark frontier?
Not death herself
but her ungentle
handmaidens.
Brittle lessons and tests
with no answers,
without choice.
A calculus of loss.
Not death but dying.

People always used to ask us, "Where did you two meet?" There is a Hollywood version of our story where Phil walks into a smoky Harlem jazz club and I'm onstage singing. He turns, and our eyes lock; it's a wrap. Love at first sight.

But that's not exactly the way it happened. What's true is that his baritone voice had me at "Hello." His voice fell on my ear and heart like music. It wasn't just what he said but the way the sound felt. At first, ours was a long-distance relationship. I was in Cambridge, Massachusetts, and he was in Durham, North Carolina. This was the seventies, pre–internet and cell phones. He'd send me cassette mixtapes with music playing in the background, and he'd just talk about his day, his hopes and dreams, and tell me how much he missed me. I absolutely loved those romantic, sweet tapes, and I'd press rewind on the tape deck over and over again. He used the song selections to help him say what he wanted to say and maybe what he couldn't say.

The songs ranged from Jeffery Osborne's "Concentrate on You" to Peabo Bryson's "Feel the Fire" to the Commodores' "Three Times a Lady." Whenever I hear these songs, they still conjure deep feelings of when we first met. This is proof positive that music is a time machine. A song can swing you right back to the very moment when you first heard it, platform shoes, shoulder pads, and all. I realized Phil was the one I'd been waiting for. He was the sound I longed to hear. Ours was a soul connection so deep it felt like a memory, like we'd met before (but of course we hadn't, at least not in this lifetime).

Phil and I actually met on July 8, 1978, on our mutual friend Bobby's front porch. It was a wonderfully steamy day in Carrboro, North Carolina. I later learned that traditional Southern porches were designed as a place of connection and community. For us, it was the grand meeting place of two souls.

There on a modest bungalow's small wooden porch we talked, and before we knew it, the sun gave way to a sky full of stars. It's likely that the crickets and tree frogs tried to join our conversation, but I could hear nothing but his voice. How could it be that we had not met before? We had been at the same wedding some years before, at the same events and parties; we had mutual friends. For over forty years we celebrated that *chance of the porch* meeting.

He said he knew right away that I was THE one. He saw our future in a flash—marriage, kids, careers, all of it. What I remember is being swept up, totally taken by this tall, handsome man. It was as if I knew him already. Well into the night we discussed everything— our families, personal histories, politics, life philosophy, hopes and dreams, favorite foods, travels—and when our talk turned to music, books, and film there was an unexpected connection. Phil asked if I'd ever heard of a film called *The Powers of 10*. Now, this film was hardly a blockbuster, and not only had I seen this nine-minute science-nerd film, but I loved Charles and Ray Eames's production. The film explored the relationships between the very huge and the absolutely tiny. By powers of ten we traveled outward from a rooftop on planet Earth to the farthest reaches of our universe. And then we zoomed inward by the same tenth powers, inside the body to the subatomic level. It was stunning that both universes—the one *out there* and the one *in here*—were so strikingly similar. To me, it helped explain a sense of order in all things and was both fascinating and spiritual.

We were astonished to find that we both loved a book called *Dune* by Frank Herbert and that our tastes in music ran the gamut from R&B to jazz to funk, including Parliament Funkadelic, Chaka Khan, James Brown, and Stevie Wonder. We spent the rest of that evening talking excitedly, remembering songs and reciting lyrics from various bands and groups we loved. Phil and I also bonded over science fiction, including *The Twilight Zone*, *Star Trek*, *The Outer Limits*, time travel, and possible futures.

We landed on our own planet, ripe for exploration. Who knew we were crafting a culture of care for each other and curiosity about a world we could build together? We discussed the living power of imagination and how important it was to change the world for the better. In that particular beginning, we'd each found the friend, the soul mate, and eventually the life partner—the lover. We kissed, and the universe kissed us back.

In the 1980s and 1990s Phil and I were busy raising three brilliant and beautiful kids, working double-time on our dreams—his architectural firm the Freelon Group and my budding career as a jazz vocalist. Phil and I created space for each other's dreams by listening to one another and by bringing every good and lovely thing accomplished in the outside world home to our hearth. It belonged to *us*. We also brought our fears, disappointments, and failures to the warmth of our family fire.

It was not easy, the coming forth of the artist, wife, and mother. I had no template for this particular path. My music called to me with as much urgency as my marriage and family. At first, it seemed that I had to choose between the two. But once I accepted dual calls, the universe began teaching me that there was less distance between paths than I imagined. Now I realize that mothering helped nurture a more organized, patient, and observant artist. And the inner artist listened and learned, navigating the creative currents inherent in music and family. I had to learn to improvise off- and onstage and found delight in becoming a weaver of my life design.

Phil and I have been referred to as a *power couple*: "You two have it all." I've always found this to be a strange descriptor of our relationship. It assumes an imbalance in relationships not described in this way. There was no need to jockey for power; it was shared wealth. What I have discovered was a truth: One could have it *all* but not *all* at the same time and, it seemed, not for *all* time.

⎯

The pulse of architecture, design, big love, and jazz music reverberated everywhere. The rhythms of practical work and the tempo of our family life felt like an improvisational dance. I learned that when jazz musicians "play outside the changes," they explore a certain tension in the music. We certainly had our share of bumps and conflicts, disturbances in the force, but we kept on moving.

By March 2016, we had started to imagine our next chapter—our children had flown from the nest, and both of our careers were on a high note. But then, a somber melody began to rise. Phil was diagnosed with ALS, also known as Lou Gehrig's disease. The doctor gave him a three- to five-year prognosis. This spelled another beginning while foreshadowing an ending.

⎯

In the fall of that same year, another beginning shimmered. The Smithsonian African American Museum of History and Culture in Washington, DC, was poised for its grand opening. As the architect of record for that project, Phil's team of Freelon Adjaye Bond had devoted over a decade to ensuring that this project would rise up from the ground before President Barack Obama left office. Phil was in every way built for this divine assignment. The building's drawings bear his architectural stamp along with his sense of pride and fulfillment. He answered the call to design excellence and the call of our ancestors, whose stories had for so long gone untold.

The jubilation was palpable as we gathered with so many at the opening of the museum in September 2016. Phil had envisioned a building that had the power to tell stories before a visitor even entered. The museum's expansive, gracious porch was a nod to the humble Southern porch and an invitation for all to be in community. On that opening day, we sensed that the throng of ancestors were well pleased with this welcoming porch place. For us, it held a deeper meaning. We kissed there, felt the humble and gracious metaphors merging, and whispered, "I love you."

I'm grateful that Phil lived to see this project through and to witness the gratitude of so many people. The opening of the museum was a glittery affair with lots of celebrities and major donors. We were brought to tears when an elderly Black gentleman smiled and said to Phil, "Well done. Well done, son." Phil's death in 2019, three years after his diagnosis, was a great loss for the design world and for his colleagues and friends. But for me, the loss was immeasurable.

It was summer, the morning your death shot through the house. Rooms emptied on your exhale. We left the windows open to an otherwise ordinary sky. And I waited for something to change, my loving you and you me. I waited until the sun slid to an orange rinse, I waited until the stars lifted their heads. I waited to feel what a difference a day makes, for the rest of the world to pour through the cracks. I waited for the widow to arrive. She was late, as I've learned is her habit. I needed her to show me how to turn the torn page.

Phil's death was totally bewildering. Why my husband? Why now? Why on the heels of great accomplishment and joy?

Phil used to talk about the existing conditions of a site or project, the findings specific to the particular design landscape that one needed to acknowledge. Maybe the site was very narrow or steep. Perhaps there was a structure nearby, or an easement. Some conditions could be altered and others not so much. In the wake of his death, I sat in consideration of my own heart's existing conditions, thinking that my forty-year life practice of loving and being loved by him had ended. I felt something groan deep inside—something for which I had no language. It was hard to describe, as if my life had become a single note ringing out, its intonation flatted by grief.

Death reveals the scaffolding that holds your heart. How had I not noticed this method of love that seeped so deeply into your marrow that you believed it to be blood-borne? I loved the story of our lives together and felt angry and disappointed about the new chapters that required a reimagination of my life without him.

This is no easy journey. It's unpredictable and requires more patience than I believed possible. There was an old gospel song I remembered, and its words reflect the mysterious nature of grace: "Grace, his grace is sufficient for victory." Grace cannot be summoned, bartered, bought, or sold. It is bestowed as a gift, oftentimes an *undeserved* one.

I've been sustained thus far not by strength, wits, bravery, or sheer willpower but by the creative power of grace. It's been a daily process, constructing new ways of being. And at times it feels exhausting. I'm reminded that Phil said, "The quality of materials used in construction is critical to its success." This is true whether you're building a house, a song, or a new life. I'm glad for the sturdy materiality of love, creativity, and grace.

NOTICE

I noticed you.
Your voice and eyes
spoke the same language.
Hello.
All my doors and windows
flew open singing yes.
I noticed the dusky
height of you,
wondered if kissing
tallness would be
a problem.
It was not.
I noticed the way
you smiled at the idea
of us together.
I noticed how
doors shimmied
with laughter.
As one by one,
children and grandchildren
rang the doorbell.
I noticed farewell
in your eyes,
could almost see
the open gate beckoning.
I noticed

how your eyes
held me until the last
possible moment.
I noticed my trembling
hinged heart
swinging
as you
brushed
past.

The business of death promised to keep me busy in ways that let me ignore my grief. There was so much to do: estate papers to fill out, insurance documents to sign, death certificates to send—the legal proof of my broken heart. Well-meaning friends offered advice, but I was too afraid to hear about things that could make it *better*. I preferred to focus on the running list of tasks, like completing the official documents, rather than listening to anyone, including Grief's intrusive voice.

My daughter suggested therapy. I resisted because, you know, listening might be involved. Friends suggested books to read. They recited time-tested scriptures. I wanted none of it. Meanwhile, Grief's voice grew stronger, threatening to overpower my internal resistance.

I considered moving, selling the house, and going somewhere else, anywhere else. Every corner held something to fear. I ached to relocate. But where? I didn't know how to shake my discomfort. The life I'd always known was gone. I yearned for a comfortable and familiar place to land. So I moved into the guest bedroom, hoping for a peace that was unavailable in the bedroom Phil and I had shared, the place where he had died. The guest bedroom didn't offer a reprieve. I already had trouble sleeping, but this room, like all of the rooms in the house, held a silence that was too loud. I tried everything, including white noise, nature sounds, meditation, and medication, but nothing offered the slightest bit of relief. Exhausted, I tossed and turned in a wearying search for rest.

Despite the so-called preparation for Phil's death, the distance between *going* and *gone* proved bigger than the Grand Canyon. And the soul silence I felt after his departure was at least that large. Everyone dies—it's part of the agreement we sign off on at birth—but not my beloved, not now, not yet. The deep voice of Grief wanted my attention, my listening ear, and I was unwilling.

I learned early on that listening is perhaps the most essential skill for a jazz musician—more important than technical know-how, vocal range, knowledge of scales or harmonic theory. It's not that these things are unimportant, but they pale in comparison to the willingness to listen deeply to the feelings at play within the music. Call-and-response is what supports an improvisational conversation, and you need to be listening to hear the call.

Yet there I was, trying my best to not hear Grief's invocation. At first, I didn't make the connection between not listening and the feeling that my voice was unavailable, remote. For me, ignoring the call of Grief came at a high cost. It meant being cut off from my muse, my inner voice. In choosing to be occupied and distracted I was also rendered voiceless.

"Hey, Nnenna," Grief whispered one day as I sifted through a mountain of papers. "Would you like to hear a story?"

"That would be a no," I thought. "I don't want to hear your story."

"My story?" Grief seemed surprised. "No, my dear, not *my story*. It's your story. Interested?"

My story? I gave myself over to the thought of it. Now that was a potent question. What kind of story is my story? A tragic tale of love and loss? A fare-thee-well story? A swan song?

As I pondered, a song began bubbling in my spirit.

So high you can't get over it
So low you can't get under it
So wide you can't get around
You gotta come in at the door.

This song spoke through my heart and loosened the stones I'd placed in my ears.

"You got to come in, sit down, and listen." That was the song's message. I began to realize, in the wake of the deaths of Phil and my sister, that I was being asked to write a new score. I didn't ask for or expect this assignment, but here it was as plain as day. And it did not sound easy at all. I wondered if I had the necessary tools for this task. My world had flipped, gone belly-up, and it was scary learning to listen again.

When I did dare listen to Grief, this is how it went:

ME: I don't know how to do this. I have no mourning experience.

GRIEF: Doesn't matter. You'll figure it out.

ME: Sounds like a full-time job.

GRIEF: It's not a job. It's an adventure and it's yours alone—you cannot fuck it up. So, if *not* listening is where you're at, then cool, go with it. Do that.

ME: Leave it to me to have a grief experience with a side of attitude.

PHIL

On the day you died
we saw a rainbow
melting into the ground.
My world tilted.
I missed you so.
The trees
showed me your face
held in their branches.
I couldn't find sleep.
An old hooty owl sang
a lullaby three nights in a row.
A hummingbird dressed like she was going to a party,
buzzing past, turned, staring
for an impossibly long time.
The wind chimes outside the back door
made a song of you when there was no wind.
The fig tree, its third year, gave exactly two figs.
One fig for you and one for me.
In the spring, a Cooper's hawk
left a perfect feather in the
middle of the walkway,
hard to miss unless
you were determined to.
A big turtle at the doorstep,
the whole entire world on her back,

looking up at me as if to say,
"Take all the time you need."
A picture of you fell out of a book
I'd never read.
You were standing at a bridge,
facing the
otherside light.

LISTENING

My sister, Deborah Pierce, was a doctor. A hospice and palliative care doctor, which meant she helped patients and their families to live well when their dying time was near. She helped people talk about things that are hard to talk about.

But most of all, she listened.

Sometimes, the patient was in pain and had been sick for a long time and wouldn't likely get any better. Deborah asked them what was important to them. She was curious about what mattered to them at that moment. She asked about their wishes and dreams.

And she listened.

Deborah listened to their stories, ones that had unfolded long before she was born. Stories about hitching a ride on a train bound for new possibilities up north, out west, anywhere but in places where your skin color determined your fate.

She listened to stories about coming to America from the old country with nothing but the clothes on their backs, and stories about the way things used to be when the world turned more slowly and *neighbor* meant something greater than proximity.

Yes, she listened.

When phrases like "she didn't make it" hung in the air like a low cloud. Or "we did all we could, but we lost him." As families were left wondering how to form new words using the past tense, she listened.

Deborah listened when an accident, suicide, or shots rang out calling loved ones' names. She accompanied the family who stood in clusters around the bed, watched the wringing of their hands as they tried to remove the smudge of the moment.

She listened to the staccato *beep beep* of monitors and the artificial trade-wind whoosh of the ventilator. Deborah knew the familiar sounds of air pushing into lungs that had forgotten the mantra "breathe in, breathe out." She listened to her patient's body, broken by circumstance. She listened to what it was saying... and what it could *not* say.

Deborah listened to the unspoken, whispered prayers and tears that had yet to fall. She listened to stories of how it happened, those terrible moments that changed everything. She heard the pleas and promises to God and angels and to those with the power to make it be okay, begging that this loss be changed to something they could accept. She bore witness to their hopes that it could be fixed and the knowledge that it sometimes just couldn't.

She listened to the anger circling around the fault lines of what someone did or didn't do. She listened to the freakish twist of fate, the ill-timed step off the curb into a crushing new life path. Deborah listened to the frustrations and questions far-flung at the gods who could allow such awful and unfair outcomes.

And she listened to the sound of the tides drifting between life and what comes next. She knew the power of machines that could stitch you to existence. And she knew their limits, the versions of life they were able to offer. When multiple meanings of life support were discussed, she listened to the nuanced meanings of those very words *life* and *support*, weighing the risk of fracture on broken and breaking hearts.

She asked the family about their loved one. What is special about them? Did they have a nickname? What was their favorite thing to do? And she listened to their replies: "Playing video games, being with family, fixing up old cars, traveling, gymnastics, gardening, sewing, playing the violin."

Deborah listened to stories that took place before she met this person, this one with whom she was now intimate but still must get to know. She was a listener to tales from a time when a different set of possibilities were in play.

She listened to treatment-weary warriors as they placed their limited options upon personal scales and watched as they tilted back and forth. Deborah listened to those not inclined to gamble—who'd never ventured to Vegas (pray for seven, come on, seven!)—bet their lives on an experimental roll of the dice. She listened in rooms where truth whispered loudly even though agreements had been signed by some not to hear. She heard the hunger for meaning where there was none—this being the sound of poverty, she listened. Deborah listened because listening was at once an act of love and an opening up of possibility.

Listening is a communal act, one that says we are knitted together and that this has always been the way of it. She knew the listener held great power to open portals of possibility. And when caught in the underwater of change, our questions bubble to the surface asking to be seen and heard. The listening heart is the medicine of the highest order. The kind of heart that belonged to my sister, Dr. Deborah Pierce.

Deborah Irene Pierce
April 13, 1958–January 5, 2020

SKIPPING

Your sister is a mirror, the reflection of your deepest self.

Lou, Lou, skip to my Lou,
skip to my Lou, my darlin'.

We would skip to school, my sister and I, happy that Mom agreed it was finally warm enough to wear just a sweater. It seemed like such a freedom to ditch the mandatory heavy coats we wore all Bostonian winter long. We skipped in rhythm along the several blocks to Russell Elementary School in Cambridge, Massachusetts. Debbie was in the third grade and I was in fourth. Skipping while holding hands requires a bit of coordination, an informal agreement that both parties will lift off and land at approximately the same time. We didn't always hold hands, but when we did, it was as if we both exercised a brief power over gravity itself. I'm trying to recall the last time I saw a kid skipping down the street. Maybe it's just too old-fashioned, or maybe I'm not hanging out on the right streets.

Skipping rope is what some folks called it, but we called it jumping or double Dutch. You needed a minimum of three people to play: two rope turners and one jumper. A knowledge of the downbeat is essential to be a good turner. We sang together, jumpers and turners, our voices mingling with the sharp slap of the rope, which was usually an old rescued clothesline. My sister was a great jumper. She, ducking in between the ropes, was jumping and turning while singing with style and grace. A lot of the songs had to do with kissing and what or who you liked or would marry.

Janey and Johnny sitting in the tree
K-I-S-S-I-N-G
first comes love, then comes marriage
then comes Janey with a baby carriage.

At that point in our young lives, we had no knowledge of such things, but we sang and laughed about that imagined grown-up world as if we did. Sadly, after a while, girls stop skipping. I'm not sure exactly when this happens or why. Maybe it has something to do with our changing bodies and high-heeled dreams. I really miss the feeling of sisterly skipping, our hands clasped together, our feet momentarily suspended above the sidewalk. It was pure joy.

Fly's in the buttermilk, shoo fly shoo
Skip to my Lou, my darling.

I wish my sister had been able to skip the diagnosis of cancer. To *shoo the fly* that threatened to spoil the sweet cream of her life. I wish all we needed to do was skip over surgery and chemotherapy and this or that experimental drug. It seemed like nothing was impossible when we held hands and skipped to school. What if, somehow, we could have defied the gravity of this moment like when we were kids?

Not long ago, I dreamt of a little girl. She was running and skipping far ahead of me. I could only see her from behind. I was thinking that it was my granddaughter and tried to catch up to her laughing frame, but I just couldn't reach her. As she turned the corner, I could see just the edge of her profile when she turned slightly, smiled, and kept moving. I smiled back at her, knowing at that moment that it was my sister Debbie, skipping off to new adventures.

MY SISTER'S ASHES

To the ocean
she said
give me back.
Shells in unison
sing welcome home.
Waves promise dances
impossible on shore.
Your currency of days
tossing in the tide
a treasure.

We adopted Basie from an animal hospital in Raleigh, North Carolina, that specializes in placing dogs with disabilities in good homes. We'd been searching for a companion dog for a while. Our requirements were simple: We preferred a female adult dog.

At the animal hospital, a happy, scruffy dog greeted me with an enthusiastic tail wag and wide canine grin. "Hello," I said, patting his head as someone called his name. When he bounded away, I noticed his missing leg. To my amazement, it didn't seem to bother him or slow him down. The receptionist took my application. It was filled with questions about our home and lifestyle. Do you own or rent? Are there young children at home? Other pets? A fenced-in backyard? How many hours will the dog be home alone? It was comprehensive.

In the past, Phil and I had always had big dogs. I remember the time the shelter folks told us that our last dog, Dexter, was an eight-month-old Beagle. They said he'd grow to 25 to 30 pounds max. That was not the case. A fully grown Dexter weighed 110 pounds and was a Greater Swiss Mountain mix. Definitely not a beagle.

Dexter died nine years after we took him home, and Phil and I felt like we'd lost our very best friend. His death came just as we downsized from 702 to our new condo. We had designed a special spot for him to be comfortable because his arthritis made it difficult for him to climb stairs, but he passed away days before we moved in. Our new condo then didn't include the canine energy that makes a house a home. We were in search of another canine friend.

A hospital tech led me to another room to meet the prospective adoptees. She introduced me to a small poodle mix. "Is he a puppy?" I asked, looking him over before reminding her of my preferences. Here was a shy, thin dog with a mass of matted, curly hair. And were those bite marks? This was not my new dog. The tech smiled and left, promising to check the other possibilities and leaving me alone with Basie.

Despite possessing all four legs, he seemed unsteady. We checked each other out from across the room. He remained in the corner, hesitant. I bent down to let him know I was a good human and encouraged him to come closer. He crouched, walked toward me, and buried his head in my lap. By the time the tech came in with another dog, it was too late. Basie and I had bonded.

Basie had been rescued from a rural shelter with thirty-five other malnourished and neglected dogs. Sadly, most of them were euthanized. Only a lucky few were adoptable. Basie tested positive for heartworm disease, and the hospital treated him with drugs and covered the cost. Since adult heartworms could get lodged in Basie's heart and lungs, he had to be quiet for the four to six weeks of treatment. At home, Basie stayed crated for most of the day. He didn't seem to mind.

Basie attuned himself to us. He learned Phil's habits and my moods. We had an incredible emotional connection. In those quiet hours, indoors for the most part and quarantined, we learned from each other, and he did not so much as bark, not once. The first time Basie did bark, it sounded like a question. Basie, so named because he could swing with the band, better than any dog or cat around, was Phil's therapy animal. Toward the end, Basie would snuggle next to Phil to give the love and reassurance that only dogs provide.

After Phil died, Basie was my constant shadow, following me from room to room. Then, on August 9, one month to the day after Phil passed, Basie died. Phil must've whistled for Basie, saying, "Come on! Good boy!" And off Basie went, like the good boy that he was.

Damn, this is too much. My dog too?

SORROW SONG

I hear you.
Been hearing you
feel your way
through it.
A dark humming

on the rise and fall
of ragged breath.
The notes you choose not to sing
ring out, strutting in their
silent dresses,
their shouting
Sunday hats.
Truths sung in the face
of a world turning away
still sound
just like
the blues.

THESE BODIES

We live in these bodies
these castles of flesh.
We die in these bodies.
Flashing past post and beam
breath and bone.
Unleashed we fly,
toward open
soul windows.
Hallelujahs clapping
as we ring past.
We live in these bodies
We die in these bodies.

February 27, 2020

Dear God,

Okay, you have all of my attention now.

After three years of heart-wrenching struggle, caring for my loving, strong, kind, and handsome husband as he withered with ALS, you *took* my soulmate, best friend, my lover. Our faithful dog Basie, who was my shadow for nine years? You took him one month later to the day, in August.

My little sister, Debbie, a skilled hospice physician, who was my armor guard through Phil's illness, who made me a big sister when I was 21 months old? You took her too.

So, yes, Lord, I am paying a high price for complete attention.

I'm hurt, angry, and confused. You took what was a beautiful and fulfilling life and left me with hardscrabble scraps. I have really tried to be the woman I thought you wanted me to be. So now, no, I don't want to hear about the goodness of the Lord. No songs about God as the promise keeper. I've lost sight of the shining path I *thought* I was on. I wonder if you are truly the trustworthy God that the old folks sang about. "Lean on him," they said. "He'll never leave you. He's a rock and my salvation." These words ring hollow in my heart now.

If you truly *knew* my heart, you'd know that I wasn't ready to say farewell to the love of my life, my best dog, and my baby sister. You'd have known how much this extravagant loss would hurt. You'd have known the unbearable ache, the unspeakable pain. And Lord, since you must've known, then HOW in the name of mercy could you allow this? Where is that grace, that sweet, sweet spirit, now when I'm in need?

I am deep in the valley of shadows where it's always midnight; the trembling quiet is my companion. I'm listening for a word from you, a word I'm not certain is coming. I've prayed for deliverance from this dark and lonely place. I can sense your hand reaching for me, yet I'm afraid, afraid to trust you when so much has been stripped from me.

I am sensing the presence of a bittersweet song, but I'm so afraid to taste. Is this what you're building up in my spirit? Lord, you must know how absolutely parched I am, how drunk with tears in this wilderness. Does my life require a new song in this strange place?

There have been occasions, onstage, in the midst of a song, when something grabs me and reaches deep inside a pocket I never knew was there. Is that you?

I don't know in these instances whether to open up a bit more or run for the nearest exit. My broken and vulnerable spirit is all I have left.

I'm listening.

GRIEF AT THE DOOR

What do you do when sorrow comes knocking? When Grief, who knows your full name and your address, is standing there, waiting for you to open the door and let her in? *Ding-dong!* There's that doorbell you don't want to answer. You've silenced your notifications, but you can still hear her begging for entry, even through the din of everyday conversation.

You could run the other way fast, but Grief is always at the finish line when you arrive, tired and sweaty. She doesn't even bother to offer you a cool towel or sip of water. You could insist that she go away, but she's stubborn and a terrible listener. As you continue to look for escape, she offers you a craggy mountain to climb, knowing you're scared of heights. You could hide, using your remaining strength to stay that way, but what good would that do?

People say you have to be strong. How? Grief's gravity is stronger than human might. She crushes you, smashing what's left of you into a million pieces. Your head hurts. Your heart hurts. It's still ticking, but the beats sound like *gone, gone, gone, gone.*

You want answers from Grief. There are none to be had. At least none that are satisfactory.

You could ignore her pestering. Act like it ain't even a thing. You could pretend to be too busy to answer her call. Sing, talk, laugh too loud, and drown out the whistling winds of sadness. You could yell through the door, "Go away" or "Come back later," or better yet, "No one's here." You could open the door just a crack. Not enough to let Grief in, just enough for a quick glimpse. You want to recognize her in case she shows up again.

Or you could suggest that you both take a walk in nature and see what the trees have to say about all this.

You could let Grief know that should you invite her in, you'd need your rest and will take frequent breaks from her difficult lessons.

Or you might say that if Grief really wants you to learn this new dance, she must remove those heavy boots and teach you the steps— SLOWLY, with patience and kindness.

Yeah. You could do that; you could certainly do that.

NOT MY LEG

My heart is broken, not my leg.
No one notices—or thinks to offer
their seat on a crowded bus.
My heart is broken, not my leg.
Strangers rarely ask: "How did it happen?"
They glance in my direction, nodding
in silent agreement.
"That must've hurt."
My heart is broken, not my leg.
Handicapped parking is off limits,
I can't risk a $250 fine.
The kid bagging groceries
doesn't ask if I need help getting to my car.
My heart is broken, not my leg.
"Be glad you have two legs"
would be rude, impolite.
Suggesting that God
doesn't give us any more
than we can handle
is not helpful or true.
My heart is broken, not my leg.
No doctor's orders,
no crutches, no plaster cast
where, if I could, I'd write
My heart is broken
not my leg.

ASSORTED BEGINNINGS

When you start to tell a story, it's probably a good idea to start at the beginning. "Once upon a time" gets you ready to listen from the point where it all began. I'm realizing, though, that grief has marked many beginnings in my life, many points in time that I can now clearly see as new chapters in the story. But here's the deal: You can only identify it as a beginning when you look back on it. It's strange, looking in the rearview mirror, your life a collection of remembered moments in time.

Since I'm less concerned with things being particularly linear, I want to start on August 21, 2017, which was the day of the solar eclipse. Phil and I made a point to go out and watch with hundreds of other folks—a singular moment, one that wouldn't come again until 2024. Seven years seemed like a really long time, and we figured this moment could be our best bet. We had no idea if we'd ever share a total eclipse together again.

I had a secret prayer that we could somehow eclipse the diagnosis of ALS and avoid what the doctors predicted would be a progressive loss of motor function leading to death. There was no cure and no real treatment. We had been told that ALS was a very rare disease, but everything is rare until it happens to you.

We decided to measure our lives by what we could do, not by what we couldn't. Phil, ever the optimist, was determined to watch the 2017 eclipse. By that time, he was using a wheelchair. We gathered in a park across the street from our downtown condo. It was really emotional watching the midday sky grow increasingly dark. It felt eerie and strange to witness the sun being swallowed up.

Where is the sun? Where is the sun?

I wondered about the early peoples, imagining what they must've thought as the sun began to disappear. Even though we had the scientific explanation as a comfort, I couldn't help but feel that the cosmic display and my personal one were the exact same thing. I remember the feeling—it was like playing the piano in the dark when the kids were little.

My practice time began after the children fell asleep. I played and sang as softly as possible, keeping the lights low so as not to wake them. Not being able to see the keys, I had to feel my way, letting the sound guide me. Each scale has a different personality, a slightly different language spoken. It was interesting getting to explore my music in this way, with my sleeping children a breath away. This, too, was the beginning of learning to hold pitches as softly as a newborn kitten, my voice a whisper in tune. I didn't know it at the time, but the improvisational thrust so important for a jazz musician was growing even then. I remember first learning a jazz standard, a Hoagy Carmichael composition called "Skylark." The story was about a bird and the search for romance. Because I was largely self-taught and my jazz conservatory was woven into my life as wife and mother of three little ones, I set the song in the soft and tender stone of a lullaby, polished with mother love. Improvisation began with a playful relationship (my kids helped me here) with melody and lyric, and it became one way to sing my three little birds off to sleep. My growing improvisational voice merged with family life. The inner artist intertwined with the mother, the wife.

I never thought of jazz music as primarily an intellectual exercise. My early exposure was through my father, who loved big bands like Count Basie and Duke Ellington. The sense of swing was bequeathed to me as I stood on the tops of his shoes dancing to "One O'Clock Jump." Dance, swing, singing, and jazz were bundled up in happiness and love.

Initially, I thought of jazz as my dad's music, but as I matured, the muse called me by my very own name. In my late twenties, I finally accepted music as my calling, my purpose in life. I wanted to become a jazz singer, yet I was a wife and a mother with very little ones. Our beautiful family was equally at the heart of my purpose. How was I to attempt a balance? Was it even possible to do both? I didn't know it then, but the answers involved becoming a weaver: taking the seemingly disparate threads of woman, wife, mother, and artist—using them to craft a living tapestry large enough to hold it all together to create another beginning.

Phil, my beloved, was there encouraging my first baby steps as I reached for the dream of becoming a jazz singer. He was a believer from the very beginning and was helping make it so while I was practicing scales, learning a new language, literally feeling my way without the blessed assurance that it'd all work out.

I'd always loved singing but never allowed myself the possibility of singing as a career. I unconsciously crafted a narrative that agreed it was impossible. And I had a mouthful of excuses—reasons why: I was married and had a family; I hadn't studied at conservatory; we lived in a small Southern town, not a jazz mecca. I became miserable and angry; my life seemed to have been already laid out. I'm sure Phil was tired of my frustration song. I remember him saying, "You can't use me and our family as an excuse for your unfulfilled dreams. If you want to sing, then do it and I'll support you." I thought, *Easy for you to say, I've got all this on me—our family* . . . but he was absolutely correct. Undressed, my excuses seemed a flimsy mask for my fears. Looking back, living my soul's purpose began simply by my finally saying "Yes."

Once I'd accepted the call to sing, the improvisational weaving began. Over and under, the threads of jazz singing intersected with family life, Phil's architectural career, and our young ones. Learning as we grew, triumphs and missteps were all visible in the tapestry of our lives. Our children grew up under theater seats and spent countless hours drawing on huge blueprint paper. Each of them has grown up to be an accomplished artist in their own right—weavers, all three.

Grief carries the coarsest of threads as I now learn to weave my life without Phil. And this weaving is as necessary as breath. The raw and unraveled, beautiful and terrible threads reach for my hands, once again asking me to say "Yes."

RESPECT

Respect. The Queen of Soul, Aretha Franklin, issued this proclamation to the world. In 1967, it reached the ears of millions and touched my Black girl's heart. This declaration, fashioned in the palm of her voice, reverberated throughout our nation—an accompaniment to the waves of people marching in the streets to demand an end to generations of racial and social grief. That song gave voice to the basic human need to be seen.

Respect. What does it really mean? We have great difficulty respecting things that we *cannot* or *will not* see. The invisible world doesn't always touch our awareness unless or until it insists on itself. The underground network of roots that lies below the surface is a complex and vast universe, many times larger than what is seen aboveground. It's an essential part of a creative whole that supports, nourishes, and actually *is* what we recognize as a flower, tree, or blade of grass. In intimate conversation, the seen and the unseen verdant world are one.

Respect requires that we *look* and *look* again more deeply. Respect calls out to us as Aretha does and bids us to spell it out—letter by letter, if necessary—to acknowledge and understand.

Grief was demanding my full attention and respect, but I believed that caring for Phil meant hiding my fear from him, from myself. In my mind, acknowledging my feelings would set us both up for a horrendous meltdown. So I set aside fears of loss and tried to untangle them from the day-to-day as best I could. It did not work, but hiding behind the mask became familiar. I was like a cloaked ship moving through Phil's journey with ALS and my sister's with lung cancer. When they died within six months of each other, the bottled-up hurt, sadness, and anger that had been begging for attention turned up the volume.

I was alone. More alone than I'd ever been in my entire life. Fears I'd carefully hidden began creeping into full view. My entire being—mind, body, and soul—was burning in Grief's fire. Split into pieces, each part of me needed something slightly different.

MY BROKEN HEART felt unprotected, vulnerable, and craved nurture, softness—someone to watch over me.

MY GRIEVING BRAIN was on overload, thinking, rethinking, making lists and safety plans. I needed a deep rest but I couldn't sleep. Awakened most nights by whirling thoughts, I lay in bed crying and fretting.

MY BODY ached with grief, and if it could have spoken aloud, it would've asked for nourishing food, more water, restorative yoga, gentle massage, walks in nature, and, if not good sleep, at least naps.

Perhaps my grief-torn spirit was sounding a call to the universe, reaching toward a world seldom seen by those unbroken by loss. What began as a gesture of respect, a willingness to look at Grief, became a space of creative engagement for my broken heart. I am a jazz singer, a storyteller, not a therapist or psychologist. My toolbox did not appear to contain anything necessary for navigation in the deep waters of loss. But what began happening was that I started to *look* and *look again* at things I'd seen but not really seen. The universe conspired to show me her wide face in every little thing. The natural world swooped, creeped, and slithered—dancing and flowing in ways I'd not noticed before. I could hear music up above my head. Flowers sang in lovely choruses; birds told me bedtime stories; dried leaves crackled underfoot, chuckling with dry humor; a hawk left me a single feather as a reminder of flight.

Out of my deep blues poured abundant narrative, song, and poetry, sometimes all at once. In respecting my Grief and her wily ways, a bigger picture began taking shape. To look and look again offered a bit of respite on this journey.

NEW RECIPE

Sadness a new recipe.
The measuring cup
makes no promise,
tells no stories
of how much
is enough,
so even its name
holds a betrayal.
The sifter, on the other hand,
favors the countless
fine grains of memory
falling
into
my
bowl.

Stolen
Moments

SECOND MOVEMENT

STOLEN MOMENTS

The Blues and the Abstract Truth—I loved that entire Oliver Nelson album. I didn't really understand the title, but I liked its invitation to let the mind wonder about what it *could* mean. The song that captured me was "Stolen Moments." It's a song where the melody gives itself over to you like an old friend at first listen. Such a treasure of symmetry with its own irresistible beauty. Not a pretty tune exactly, but regal and sure of itself. The notes are arranged as a completely satisfying story. I found myself annoyed with the vocal versions of the song. As much as I would have loved to have stood onstage, head cocked to one side, microphone in hand, with that royal melody rising in my throat and some hip words to tell a story with it, I was like, nah, that's just not it . . . at all, period.

You see, I'd already claimed deep feelings of my own articulated in the melodic strut. The song was pure eloquence beyond words. Grief and time have a queasy relationship. On the one hand, it's clear that she (Grief) doesn't relate to time as we do. None of the yardsticks we use to measure apply.

On the other hand, Grief has by her very presence taught me so many lessons on the subject. Stealing time, as in the old Negro spiritual "Steal Away," has always been an enigma. As a kid, my parents taught us not to steal—it was wrong to take something that didn't belong to you. And there we were, in church no less, singing about stealing?

Steal away, steal away,
Steal away to Jesus!
Steal away, steal away home,
I ain't got long to stay here.

I remember a minister preaching on this very subject. His main point seemed to be that if you were stealing *to Jesus*, and not *from Jesus*, then that made it all right. It was a holy gesture. My little child's mind wondered, *Why stealing? Why not just step up nicely? Or kneel patiently?*

Later, I learned how his message rode around the facts of a people living under the yoke of slavery and ignored their use of coded song as a real form of resistance. When your choices are not your own, to risk *stealing* them is a valid option. Why else would it be stated no less than five times in the first verse? It is a shout-out to listeners to wrestle whatever chance at freedom and run. When Grief speaks to my heart of *time stealing*, it has more to do with snatching moments from the calendar of days, the watch, and the ever-present iPhone. These time-pieces are tools that can tell you only *particular* stories. "It's been two years since he passed" or "It's been so long, I should be feeling better."

Grief knows that there are other stories besides the ones time can tell, and she's forever trying to show me. Nature, for example, holds places where one can be lost in time. Her ways are stealthy, slowing me down and focusing the eye and mind on tiny things. Things I'd surely miss otherwise.

The ants in lockstep are marching busily about their ant business. They give their undivided and full attention to the task at hand. When I interrupt the path with a stick, they seem to hesitate and make decisions. Left or right? Backward or forward? And then, with the best choices made, they keep it moving... on with the show.

Observing these tiny teachers, I'm impressed with how they viewed the obstacle in their path. Maybe it was my imagination, but it seems like they were curious: "Can we go over this thing? Around? Through it?" They finally (most of them anyway) decided to go around and resumed the path they'd been on before.

Grief bade me notice these little ants. I towered above them and on a usual day, busy with human business, had never taken the time to really *see*, to be in consideration of ant life.

Grief made me curious, and I was happy to become a momentary pickpocket, catching the common coins fallen from an ordinary day. Maybe it is the inelegant breaking that makes your heart long for these nearly invisible gifts. It almost seemed like they'd been waiting to be seen: a hawk circling on a curtain of wind; in groups of three, mossy stones perfectly arranged; ants on parade, making the best choices possible given their circumstances. Stolen moments? Yes, please! I'm all about snatching a few extraordinary threads from the hem of the day.

ON BE COMING

"She'll Be Coming 'Round the Mountain When She Comes"

Arrival.

This is not a trip I'd planned. Usually, when I have to travel, I purchase my ticket at the best price possible. Sometimes *best* means a direct flight, shortening my overall time on the road. And so the best is not always cheapest. If someone else is buying my ticket and it's more than four hours by plane, I insist on business class. There is a well-loved saying: "I play for free. I get paid to travel." Time spent in TSA lines, hotels, airport lounges, cars, awaiting ground transport vans, buses, and trains—all of this is a part of life on the road. A part of a life I have chosen and love despite the challenges. But this nonconsensual trip of sorrow was thrust upon me.

No overpacking the suitcase with things I decide are needed and end up not using. No research on the average temperatures, major cities, social customs, languages, or cultural mores—none of the travel stuff—is helpful for this journey. It was just me staring out at this vast territory without a compass or a map.

Let's begin with a few deep breaths in and out.

I recall my yoga breath practice being helpful when I felt anxious. But even the deepest belly-expanding breath (imagining my back body filling with air) did no good. My heart was still quaking. Is this what grief is? Is this what heartache feels like?

She'll BE *coming 'round the mountain when she comes . . .*

This song. Why is this song ringing in my head? Is grief stimulating auditory hallucinations? I bet I hadn't thought about this song in over fifty years. It was a camp song, a kids' song, of course; I knew it, but what did it have to do with my current situation as a new arrival on grief's rocky shores?

She'll be coming 'round the mountain could be a metaphor for a lot of things. Am I the *she* of whom the song speaks? Is the distant mountain the craggy and steep one that I'm to climb? And why the use of repetition? To be certain I get it? Three times for good measure?

The song kept replicating, showing up again and again, and try as I might, I couldn't shake it. And so I did what anyone with a computer might do—I searched the internet.

The song we know as "She'll Be Coming 'Round the Mountain" was first published in 1899. However, the melody was *borrowed* from an old Negro spiritual called "When the Chariot Comes." This *chariot* was not born of idle curiosity; it asked an intentional question crafted from the dreams of liberation. Who will drive the chariot—that sweet chariot destined for freedom? It was a song of hope and promise, a song emerging from a people's painful experience. And one conjuring a future, engaging the imagination of another place, another time. This song was a rejection of their current reality and a reimagination of *being*.

I was enthralled with this musical mashup of driving chariots and big mountains, and of the idea of a powerful *she* who the song promised was on her way, coming and becoming.

I never knew the roots of this song and its connection to ancestral grief, hope, and resilience. Grief tilted my world on its axis and made me feel porous, open in new ways. Perhaps it was always tilted a bit, like our planet on an axis of 23.4 degrees, in a galaxy rushing out at 2.2 million kilometers every hour, while at the same time 2,000 gallons of air passes through my body and what I ate for breakfast was being transformed—that banana, on its way to becoming something new. At times it was bewildering, but I was made more aware of everything being in constant flux. I was at the mouth of sorrow's journey, tilting, with no map and a kids' song ringing in my ears, one borrowed or stolen from an old Negro spiritual.

Technology. Yes, technology. We don't think of a song as being tech. We've become accustomed to the idea of technology being embodied in devices that we hold in our hands. But wait: If we define technology as something that changes the way we think and do, something that creates new modes of energy transfer, reaches out and touches our beingness—then song, art, dance, music, storytelling, all of this is indeed by definition technology. And so is meditation, prayer, and mindfulness, too.

You and I weren't there on the day the songwriter flung a power-filled questioning thought into the song and let it fly. Who will drive the chariot not *if* but *when* she comes? We were not members of that humble choir who dared pose this audacious question through the technology of song and pressed it against their anguish.

Who will drive the chariot when she comes?
Who will drive the chariot when she comes?
Who will drive the chariot?
Who will drive the chariot?
Who will drive the chariot when she comes?

The two songs tumbled over and over in my head, and after a while, a realization led to an inner smile . . . I'm the recipient!

***

What I'm hearing is an automated ancestral message sent from the 1850s disguised as a kids' song to point me toward hope. Me, a twenty-first-century wayfaring stranger in the parallel universe of grief, a new believer in be coming.

THE TRAIN

I've always been fascinated by trains. I grew up in the Boston area, and the subway trains used to delight and scare me. It was dark and musty underground, and the older trains were very loud. I still have a recurring dream where I'm scrambling at the platform and it starts to tilt down toward the tracks. And another one, where someone is pushing me way too close to the yellow line. I'm frightened of falling onto the third rail and ending up like the cartoon image of the guy painted on the rail, his feet and arms twisting in the air beneath the yellow letters warning DANGER: LIVE RAIL! I always wake up relieved that it was only a dream.

There's something powerful about train imagery. When I was little my grandmother took me on my very first overnight trip. We were going down south to St. Louis to visit her sister, and we took the train. It was early-morning dark when we left, and what I remember most was the train itself, which to me looked like a huge beast breathing steam. It was scary and thrilling at the same time. We found our seats and I got to sit by the window. Watching the world stretch out from Boston to St. Louis is something I'll never forget.

So many people came and went. Some folks had friendly conversations with my grandmother, talking about their families, the weather, or where they were headed, and some were silent as a stone. When they got to their stop, these strangers nodded goodbye or left without a word.

After a while I became much more curious about when it'd be our turn to get off the train. Grandmother said it'd be two days before we got there, but to me, it seemed much longer. By the time we did arrive, I'd made a few friends along the way. One was a girl about my age—we'd been sitting together giggling and playing. When the conductor announced, "St. Louis!" I was happy but also a little sad to leave my new train friend. It was our turn to say goodbye and leave the other passengers to wonder where we were going. My grandmother and I gathered our things and stepped off. The rest of the trip is a blur in my memory, but riding on the train is imprinted in my spirit.

The thought of the train as a metaphor for living has been super helpful in my grief journey. We're all on this life train. Everyone has a ticket with a specific destination. We don't know where or when it's going to be our turn to get off the train. All we know for certain is that everybody gets to do it. No exceptions. We don't know exactly where we're going when we depart, nor can most of us remember where we were before we got on board. This is one of life's greatest mysteries.

New people get on all the time, babies, partners, friends, and enemies. Some are super close, occupying the seat right next to us, and when they depart that seat feels so very empty. Others we barely know take their leave and it feels like a whisper. There are times when you get a chance to say your goodbyes—thanking them, wishing them well—and other times you look away and *whoosh* they're gone.

I remember reading a book called *The Platform Ticket* when my mother neared the end of her life. It talked about the dying waiting on their train. We as caregivers, friends, and family have what's called a platform ticket. It allows us to stand alongside the dying, reassuring and tarrying with them until their train arrives. The platform ticket gives us permission to accompany the dying but not to board the train. When the time comes, they step aboard into the big mystery, and we are left to wave goodbye and perhaps wonder where they've gone. It was a good book for my caregiver's soul, offering a real sense of purpose to my role, which at the end of Mom's life consisted of comforting and waiting with her.

Phil created a playlist for his end-of-life journey. The song "Last Train Home" by Pat Metheny was one of his favorites. There were songs by some of his favorite artists, like "Zoom" by the Commodores, "Going Up Yonder" by Walter Hawkins, "Shining Star" by Earth, Wind & Fire, and my recording of "I Say a Little Prayer." Choosing the songs for his departure playlist was his way of making peace with his train's approach and saying goodbye. I haven't listened to Phil's playlist since he passed away, but I know the songs by heart. Whenever I hear a song from his list playing on the radio, it feels like he's paying me a very special visit. It's just one more way that he lets me know he's saving a seat for me in first class when it's my turn to ride that train.

BALM

I've read that in some traditions, the newly dead's name is not to be spoken out loud lest they be disturbed and turn toward the world of the living. After the first year of mourning, it is okay to speak of them, as they have, by then, become fully acclimated to their new world.

I didn't know about this practice until recently, but even if I had, it would have been very hard for me to follow those rules. I said Phil's name loudly and often. I sought his counsel, played music we both loved, sang to him, cried his name into my pillow—all of that and more. I hope my daily reach wasn't a pain in the ass for him, because I did call a brother's name . . . a lot. I missed him in this world. How could I resist?

Phil's death seemed like an awful trick—a mistake. When my sister died in the midst of my fresh mourning, I honestly felt numb. These compound losses threatened everything I thought I believed, leaving me angry and guilty—especially about my capacity to mourn my sister.

My faith was on trial. I doubted everything I'd been told about the "goodness of the Lord." Having grown up in a church where mourning was as necessary as it was sacred, I reached for the sense of community ritual in songs. But I found the songs hollow, the mourner's bench too hard and lonely.

"Precious Lord, Take My Hand"

How many times had I sung this song at funerals? How many times had the Holy Spirit come through like sonic vapor? Even before I knew how completely the word *precious* would describe my own personal losses, I sang this heartsong and felt its earnest plea. Now, crumpled by the weight of grief, I knew the hard truth living at the lyric's center: *Take my hand* was not a request; it was the begging of the soul in the wilderness.

Blessed are they who mourn, for they shall be comforted.
— MATTHEW 5:4

I memorized the Beatitudes as a child but never thought my life would give me sufficient reason to question the validity of the sermon.

No, this did not feel like a blessing at all. Was I being punished? Singled out for a supreme test of faith?

I railed at a mighty God who gives and takes away without mercy or loving-kindness.

Amazing grace / How sweet the sound / That saved a wretch like me.

The only part of this song that resonated was the wretch part. I wondered if it was possible to sing with a mouth full of ashes. I was now the wretched one. This felt like an impossible grace, and where was that sweet, sweet spirit?

There is a balm in Gilead / To make the wounded whole

A wanderer in grief's Gilead, in search of a balm—a healing. I recorded this song in 2005 on my CD *Blueprint of a Lady*. But I could no longer view it as an affirmation of belief. My sorrow had transformed belief into a host of questions. *Is there no balm in Gilead?* Is there no medicine for my broken heart?

———

I slept with my body curled in a fist. Some mornings I'd awaken with my jaws aching from the all-night clench of anger and fear.

———

"Look. Come to the edge of the abyss and look."

———

Was this the Holy Spirit? Or God herself checking in on a sister?

The last thing I wanted was to look at the enormity of my loss. To stare down the throat of a life without Phil, without my sister Debbie, without my dog Basie? No, thank you very much. But again it resonated.

—

"Look. Come to the edge of the abyss and look."

—

Persistence. Spirit is nothing if not that. I felt it, something leading me to the precipice and bidding me to open my eyes and heart. I was resistant. After all, what was there for me to see, to own, but losses stacked one on top of the other?

—

I wouldn't. I couldn't. I folded my arms, in a flat-out refusal of the invitation to clamber up these stark cliffs.

—

A little over a year after Phil passed, we decided to revive our traditional family Thanksgiving. In years past, kids and grandkids would gather at our home. The house was filled with lots of laughter and the smells of yeast rolls and sweet potato pie. Phil and I happily presided over the feast. He would remark, "It comes in handy to have an architect carve your turkey." But this year, it was difficult. The joys of family seemed like presents I could not open.

We always said a blessing before eating, remembering those who no longer sat with us, and then we'd go around the table, starting with the youngest, each one saying what they were thankful for. I knew this time I'd be the last to offer thanks, and to be honest, I was having a hard time shifting my focus to gratitude. I considered asking to be excused just this one time, but I thought it would set a bad example for the young ones, so I decided to offer a vague, quick thanks and be done with it.

The night before, as I meditated on something to say that wouldn't set off an avalanche of tears, a blooming began inside. I closed my eyes, took a deep breath, and asked myself, "What are you grateful for?" A simple question, right? Suddenly, all the emotions and lived experiences that made my life golden, precious, came thundering out. My heart had been so heavy, and some of that weight was, surprisingly, gratitude. Once begun, thank-yous kept rolling out like a river—a river that carried me all the way to the edge of the very abyss that I'd been avoiding. I was amazed to find myself there—it was never my intent to travel to that appointed place. Yet, there I was, trembling, breathless, and . . . surprised.

A divine presence spoke gently to my heart. "Come," she said. "Open your eyes. Don't be afraid."

"Trust me, you are so loved."

It took everything within me to open my eyes on the dizzying mount of my grief. I expected emotional vertigo, standing at that blustery height, but what I felt was something else. It was strangely beautiful and nearly impossible to describe. Instead of a dark void it was full of light and joy. It was as if I could for a split second see all of creation in a divine dance where absolutely nothing is lost.... *Nothing*.

Colors and patterns, some dark, some light, were all woven together in a patchwork of great beauty. Some gentle nudge of the heart said, "There are some things you can only witness from this vantage point." I watched in wonderment as I felt my beloved Phil surface like a dolphin. He smiled so playfully and warmly. There was no pain, no ALS, no limits to his connection with everything else in the universe. My heart leapt with the joy. This was a flash of insight, a bit of grace inside a meditative dream, not a pretty bow to tie upon the enormity of my losses. Yet it was beautiful, to get a tiny glimpse of what else is possible beyond our rational understanding.

Balm in Gilead, I sing the minor affirmative blues, the verse adorned with stripes of joy and pain.

Sometimes the question and the answer lie in the same unpredictable symmetry.

THERE IS A BALM IN GILEAD

African American hymn

*There is a balm in Gilead
To make the wounded whole
There is a balm in Gilead
To heal the sin-sick soul.
Sometimes I feel discouraged
And think my work's in vain
But then the holy spirit
Revives my soul again.*

THE WEDDING

Nobody ever says you need a brand-new résumé when your spouse dies. This fact is never discussed in grief counseling. If I had still had a typewriter, it would have been good to be able to sit and ponder, perhaps with a cup of mint tea, while sliding paper into the IBM Selectric. I could have used some gentleness, a thoughtful ritual of some sort, in this hard-edged moment. But this grief-attenuated rewrite of my résumé holds no ease. It's hard enough to consider thorny questions like "Who am I?" for myself, let alone for others. It stinks to have had your name changed without your permission. *Widow*. Like it or not, that's technically what they call folks whose husbands have died.

Nova, my five-year-old granddaughter, asked me, "Giva, are you wedding?" Now with this one, I had to inquire and get a bit more information before giving an answer. I tried to read her face, which was a mix of 50 percent quizzical, 30 percent shy, and a tiny smidge of embarrassment.

I replied, "Are you asking me if I'm *going* to a wedding or if I've *had* a wedding?"

"No," she said, slightly louder and with more confidence. "I'm saying... Are you *wedding*?"

Hmm, I thought, *she's using* wedding *as a verb*. What an interestingly creative question. Kinda like "Giva, are you *still wed* to Pop Pop?" I'm pretty sure she doesn't know the word *widow* or what it means. I haven't used the word to describe myself, nor has anyone else, to my knowledge. She knows her Pop Pop, my husband Phil, has died. She understands he's everywhere but that we can't see him or touch him. I'm sure she misses his presence and she knows I miss him too, especially the touching and seeing him part. To be sure I understood the question, I said, "Are you asking me if I'm married?"

She looked at me like I was either hard of hearing or something akin to not too smart.

"No, Giva," she sighed, tired of my playing the dolt. *"Wed-ding! Are YOU wedding?"*

I carried that question around in my heart like a lucky penny. What a fine question my genius grandgirl had posed. With a smile broadening at the thought, I asked myself, *Am I? Still wedded, that is.* I fingered my wedding bands and engagement ring, remembering when Phil and I renewed our vows on our twenty-fifth anniversary. We gathered in our home surrounded by our three children, our family, and friends as we made fresh promises to love and honor each other until "death do us part." He surprised me with a new sparkly ring, one which, he said, symbolized how much our love had grown over the years. After Phil died, I retrieved the cherished ring he'd placed on my finger in October 1979 and decided that now, I'd wear all three rings.

I promised on that day to love him until death parts us. However, given the present circumstances, I decided to gladly break that promise. I will love Phil *through* death, his and my own. I will continue to wear my rings, laugh with him, seek his counsel, and honor and cherish our lives together. I get to love him forever while being his beloved.

So, in answering my little granddaughter Nova's question "Giva, are you wedding?," my answer is "Yes, absolutely, I certainly am."

SILENCES

Once again, they've come.
The throng of silences,
arrive on tiptoe.
Each one carries
a silken drawstring purse.
Their gloved hands
point toward my ruby throat,
to the thick coating of lost words clinging
to the roof of my mouth.
Fingers press against my lips.
They taste like shame and fear.
Bitter.
I lick them anyway.
Swallow.
Pitch deep,
in my marrow
I hear
unsung islands
growing.

THE MOON AND ME

My grandmother, Irene Perry Smith, was born in Bonita, Louisiana, in 1899. She did not believe that anyone had landed on the moon. She thought the lunar landing was a hoax—end of story. She believed in God, the Holy Spirit, working hard, getting a good education, heaven, hell, and the power of prayer. But when it came to men walking on the moon, her mind was made up. It didn't happen.

When I was little, it seemed like the moon and I had a thing going on. I knew she liked me because she followed me wherever I went. I kept this fact to myself because I didn't want anyone else to feel bad that she was playing favorites. It was our secret, the moon and me. One day, I let it slip, our arrangement—the one where she always followed me. We were riding in the car and I was staring out of the window, marveling at how cool it was that the moon followed our car and, more specifically, our car with *me* in it. My brother laughed out loud, using the words *optical* and *illusion* like hot pokers. "The moon," he said, in an older-brother smarty-pants way, "appears to follow everybody." He didn't use the word *dummy*, but the tone of his voice pointed in that direction.

In that instant, I knew he was right, and I was crushed that I could've been so mistaken. Years later, when we huddled around the black-and-white TV watching the astronauts walk on the lunar surface, I thought about that time in the car, about the feeling of having a secret celestial love and how special that was.

It feels very personal now that the moon is my grief partner.

In recent days, we've reconnected around my losses. And I've found the moon to be good company; her conversations make lonely nights a little less so. Even in her new-moon self, clothed in darkness, she demonstrates the need for deep rest. Oh, how I need this reminder to offer myself this gentle gift of kindness. On nights when she is growing toward fullness or heading offstage to replenish, we'd sometimes discuss music and how long it might take for the moon song to reach me. And she'd say something like "My full cycle from rest to rest is about twenty-nine or so of your days. Songs are always coming and going and coming again." Ah, the lunar resonance offers such clarity in the night. Everything, all the time, in ways seen and unseen, ever coming and going.

THE TURTLE

I thought it was a stone. That's what it looked like from my bottom-of-the-hill vantage point. It was a large stone in the middle of the driveway that hadn't been there last night. Upon approach, it began lumbering slowly up the hill, so I figured it couldn't be a stone, at least not the normal kind. The stone was actually a turtle. She stretched her bespeckled neck, observing me, opening and closing her mouth so that it looked like a pair of old green pliers. *Was she yawning? Was I boring? Was she trying to communicate?*

Clearly, she didn't consider me a threat as she continued holding me with her alien eyes.

Finally, needing to attend to more pressing matters, she stretched her surprisingly long legs and propelled herself forward. Whatever was calling her must've been something very important, even essential. Hers was a wheel-of-life survival energy.

She must, I thought, be searching for a place to lay eggs.

Why not lay them where you spend most of your days and nights? I wondered. Why not squirt them out in that same water, in numbers high enough to ensure that some will survive? A gamble for sure, but certainly not one greater than this gamble, which involves climbing my driveway in broad daylight and risking being run over by my Subaru. Her eggs also share in this dangerous venture. Even if she finds a suitable spot to bury them, they could still become a tasty meal for raccoons or foxes.

The turtle kept it moving, paying no mind to my musings about her fate, turtle futures, survival rates, and alternative egg-laying strategies.

She was, in every sense, playing the hand she was dealt. Climbing the hill may have played only a bit part in the script of her life. Her face betrayed no emotions. If she was frustrated or annoyed—angry with her assignments—I could not tell. And the large numbers of turtles lined up on half-submerged trees in the lake suggested this ancient plan was working well for them.

What if I could do what the turtles do—without judging myself or resisting—and just play my own hand? Just read the cards of fate spelling out this part of my life that feels like lumbering up a steep hill.

I'm sure the turtle was tired. It was a long, slow, hot climb. Following her, I watched as she reached a mossy patch. She stopped, unperturbed by my nosiness. Breathing heavily? (I'm no expert on turtle breathing, but it seemed that way to me.) She rested a bit, gathering herself. In a few moments, presumably restored, she stretched her legs and resumed her mission. Not once did she look back at the road she'd already traveled. Some deep calling urged her ever forward; some song whose melody I wished was in the range of my hearing was playing. I watched until she disappeared beneath a mass of leaves and twigs. There, in the cool and dark canopy of trees, I thanked her for a powerful moment in my own grief journey. I wished her well and hoped she could find a safe nest for her belly full of eggs.

CRICKET

Grief expands and contracts like planetary bellows. There's no way to predict her rhythm—to anticipate the surge and maybe dodge that awful heat. She dresses up for birthdays, holidays, or death anniversaries—but she also arrives unannounced in the robes of an absolutely ordinary day. Trying to plan for her outbursts is impossible. I've found myself answering the call to *regular* life and feeling pretty damn good about it, only to find myself melting in an unexpected, sudden heat wave.

Among a great many other things, Grief's attention made me feel small and vulnerable. My universe, until recently, included one beloved life. That one flickering candle out of nearly seven billion people was extinguished, and my entire world became a shrunken apple.

It's October. The days are cooling and nights are lengthening. I wonder aloud how to make it through winter's dark embrace. I search in vain for a frame of mind that can hold the cadence of winter without Phil and find nothing in my repertoire. Nothing at all.

—

Today, something in my house cut through the quiet with serrated chirping sounds. I looked around, searching for some flirting in the shadows. The moment I approached, the sound rippled to a stop. It sounded like a cricket, but this late in the season?

The cricket chorus that lulled me to sleep on summer evenings was long over, and that concert was definitely conducted outside the house.

Somewhere, I read that finding a cricket in your home was a sign of good fortune. Therefore, you should not kill or remove it, as you'd deny yourself the good luck it brings. If this was a cricket, I sure could use some.

Again, a *chirp chirp*. A cricket singing this late in the year?

I approached the sound and waited; when it began to sing again, I slowly lifted a chair leg and discovered a very small brown cricket wedged in the corner. Captivated and curious, I tilted into its story. Crickets are nocturnal (these days we have that in common). All the singers happen to be male, rubbing their wings together with the intention of attracting a mate. Apparently, crickets were the first to profess their love through song. This fascinating rhythm is 300 million years old.

I was struck by the risky business of chirping. What if something with an appetite for crickets were to hear? Maybe he could leap out of danger and live to sing another day, but maybe not. He began earnestly chirping again and I felt a wave of envy. In my imagination, my lover called out to me, loudly proclaiming that no other in the world would do. It'd be impossible to resist his charming and finely tuned melody. But what was actually happening was that a little brown cricket was singing a lonely solo in a dark corner of my living room, out of season, with no female within earshot.

The cricket's story and my own were intertwined. We both longed for our beloved. My ears (affixed in the customary place) and my cricket friend's (located behind his knees) listened for the hint of love between chirps. Lost in thought and meticulously preserved, the silence between chirps held the sound of October's heart breaking.

DWELLING

I dwell in the house of grief
telling myself that the move is just temporary
That one day I will find residence
in finer climes
For now it is a shuttered palace
Dinner: rice with no beans or beans with no rice
The chef here is lazy
She knows only the recipes of loss
and
carefully she measures what isn't there
omitting all the goodness of spice
She claims that dining on the missing helps to reveal
the main ingredient
I believe she has no talent for
cooking
Memories stalk the halls
shaking their bobble heads
left and right
searching for evidence
that your departure is the stuff of dreams
Every morning the furniture is rearranged
Again and again
I stub my toe on the corner
of what was ...
Dishes wait in the sink
The crust is now days old

Too hard to scrub with bare fingers
The chef is experimenting
with a new recipe
This time, beans and rice without either
"Less is more!" she says cheerily
I'm too tired to attempt
an argument over nothingness
The dishes, I think, will be a momentary distraction
But no

CONTAINER GARDEN

My kitchen garden is right by my back door. Every time I go in and out I'm greeted by herbs and veggies nestled in their pots. They offer green beauty to my eyes and inspire with mouth-watering scents. Sometimes they speak to me, saying they're glad to be alive or perhaps a bit thirsty, and, other times, they offer menu suggestions: "How'z about pesto for dinner? Herby omelet?"

Well, they don't always speak; sometimes they just nod and go back to their green business. These potted lovelies have taught me so much about grieving. One thing I'm noticing on this journey is that anything—literally anything—you turn toward has a message to share, and it's yours and yours alone.

Nature especially has a lot to say. The natural world is doing cartwheels to get my attention. The full moon leaning her head down on my pillow, spilling moonmilk all over the bed... brilliant sunsets with impossible pinks and purples, the clouds joining in with deep streaks of blue.

I never remember witnessing such strange beauty before Phil passed. Perhaps these signs were always there and I didn't notice. A big ol' turtle carrying her entire world on her back, neck stretching to look me straight in the eye, saying, "Take it slow, sister. This thing ain't a race. Take all the time you need." And this year, more roses than I've ever seen in my life.

See, there was a rosebush in the yard that I'd planned to dig up this year. I planted it the year Phil passed. It was looking so poorly last summer, with yellowed leaves and bare branches. Every time I looked at it, it made me sad.

First thing in the spring, I said to myself, I'm going to dig it up and plant a new one. Well, I'd forgotten about my promise to dig it up, and lo and behold! This spring, up jumped so many, a rodeo of roses deep red, vibrant. The bouquet bush is so heavy it's leaning over, and more are coming. I'm feeling like Phil is smiling. Everything's coming up roses.

I'm learning such interesting lessons from my kitchen garden.

Containers

The pots for one thing. Now, I love a pretty pot dripping with color with a wide and welcoming mouth. Or the tall and narrow stately one, the gentle sloping bowl-shaped, the gracefully curved clay pot decorated with vibrant colors, each one a distinct personality.

But I also love alternative containers, things that can work so nicely to hold the soil and make a home for a plant—plastic buckets, old toys, even a fireplace grate can behold possibility.

The repurposed containers spark my imagination, but I have also been known to buy a gorgeous pot just because, without the slightest notion of what will go inside of it.

The different shapes and sizes are speaking a specific medicine to my heart. Each one holds space—a particular kind of environment for growth. It's certainly not one-size-fits-all. I've had many a plant wither away, unhappy with my choices of soil, light, water, and pot size.

I have a collection of tiny terra-cotta pots. Not more than two inches tall. They aren't big enough for anything that needs to stretch out. No carrots or tomatoes growing here. These are unsuitable for a deep-rooted plant but perfect for the dainty, I'm cool, chilling here kind of seedling or plant.

I've lined them up like little soldiers. Sometimes, I move them around and make groupings of different shapes. Because they're so small, they need to be watered more regularly than my big pots. It takes about thirty seconds and we're done.

They're saying to my heart, "One little bite at a time. I'll hold these tiny moments for you, and I promise not to get any bigger or die off if you care for me here in my little world." I find there are everyday trifles that need holding on my grief journey. Like a well-meaning comment from a friend or loved one about their grief journey that feels ... not helpful.

A small thing perhaps, but it still needs careful tending, or you could be tempted to transplant it to a bigger pot where it would very likely flourish.

Basil is the queen of my kitchen garden. Who knew there were so many different kinds, each one with its own particular vibration. Sweet basil is the kind I was most familiar with. I've grown it indoors in a sunny spot, and it's been happy to provide the flavors of summer well into early winter. Recently, I've been introduced to Ethiopian holy basil, also called *besobela*. Curious, I bought seeds from an artisan seed company. This plant is truly a medicine plant. Every part of her is a gift. Her leaves scent butter and flavor stew, her flowers attract bees, and dried along with lavender she invites a restful sleep.

All a sister wants in return is sun, lots of it. I watch *besobela* leaning into the rays, growing taller, stretching to get just a little bit more of that good solar energy. What powerful lessons for me from this African basil, to stretch with my face to the sun.

Grief benefits from containers, from places where it can safely be with offerings of nourishment and nurture. Places where we can tend to the parts that hurt. I've also found containers to be arenas of divine play and creativity. The container is where I set my intentions around joy and mourning. My containers—cooking, gardening, listening to music, writing—allow me to DO the particular work that I feel called to do in my healing.

My musical creative life, where I journey to improvise, sing, and play, always brought me great joy. In my early grieving this place seemed very off-limits. My singing voice was unavailable, foreign. The stunted sprigs of my former self lay in waste. I was afraid to dig around in that pot, afraid . . . lest I be consumed, buried, or, worse, find it totally emptied out by my grief. *Ahhhh.*

Be it large and small, decorative or plainly made, containers—good and right-sized ones—help keep grief from becoming all-encompassing.

—

Now we must speak of mint. It said clearly on the instructions to plant in a container lest it spread out weedlike and invade the entire garden. Mint, they cautioned, needs a container. Well, I, being a lover of adult beverages mingled with mint, did not see the danger in this very small potted plant. I imagined it growing nicely and providing me with fresh adornments for drinks like my husband's fave Moscow mule.

I learned a not-so-subtle lesson about grief through my mint experience. Sooner than I would have thought possible, mint was everywhere. Growing vertically, sideways, and overtaking everything in its path. Where I had visions of mint *in* my garden I now had a garden of only mint. I dug up clumps of mint quite a far distance from where I originally planted it. This is why, I discovered, mint needs to be contained. Grief also has a spreading habit, runners moving underground until there's little life space available. Containers allow a bit of grace, a space to tend and allow growth without pushing out all the other things life offers.

My podcast *Great Grief* and the decision to write this book didn't start with my desire to be a writer or podcaster. I certainly do not consider myself an expert. It started out as a very small container—my personal journals. Into it I poured questions, heartache, joy, anger, fear, anxiety, and memories. Tear-stained pages held the stories of my brokenness. I couldn't write fast enough to keep up. After a time, I began recording, speaking into my voice memos on the phone and singing original melodies of joy and sorrow. The daily practice of storytelling to my own heart gave me a place of healing.

After a long time, the energy outgrew its original container and needed repotting. *Great Grief* the podcast and this book, *Beneath the Skin of Sorrow: Improvisations on Loss*, became new containers. I'm realizing now that tiny seeds of joy, peace, curiosity, and wonder have begun to take root. This abundant energy stirred by my grief walk transformed the personal into the universal. I didn't do this any more than I can claim to make herbs grow.

And I'm so very grateful for this moment in time where I can see a hint of flowering in these strangely beautiful pots of great grief.

DRY TOAST

Of days
dark and brittle
slightly burned
on one side.
Isn't this what
we serve
to sick people?
Give to prisoners
as punishment?
I've been churning
for a long while
and nothing's risen
to the top.
No buttery laughter,
thickened memory.
Seems like I should
have by now,
some gay
spread.
"Keep churning."
She said,
"It takes
as long
as it takes."

ONIONS

Part One

This is a story about onions and love—self-love.

I read somewhere that the tears you cry when you chop onions are not the same as the ones you shed when you are emotional. Not exactly sure about the differences, but suffice it to say that scientists have studied them and there is a difference.

Phil didn't like onions. This is a point he made clear when we were dating. He had had some bad experiences with them. Like being forced to eat them and not being allowed to explain that it wasn't the dish that he didn't like, it was the onions in the dish. I don't know. I forget all the details but the short of it is this: No onions for Phil.

I, on the other hand, love onions and always have. I love them grilled, fried, sautéed, pickled, raw. I just like 'em. I like the whole onion family: Vidalia, red, scallions, leeks, all of them.

Well, here's a bit of a problem. Food is my love language and my husband doesn't like onions, so I practiced onion avoidance. I either didn't use them if a recipe called for them, or I chopped them so fine and didn't tell him. (He didn't notice.) Or I did some other sneaky onion subterfuge, usually with good results. Phil said it wasn't that he disliked the way onions tasted; it was a texture thing. Big, slimy chunks were the problem. So I resorted to onion powder, onion salt, or granules.

I wonder how many breakfasts, lunches, and dinners added up to forty years. How many times did we eat out? I know whenever he ordered a sandwich it was "No onions, please." And if onions mistakenly ended up on the sandwich? They were meticulously picked off and tossed in the trash.

When Phil passed away, there was a long period when I had no interest in cooking, with or without onions. There were many, many tearful days and nights, none of which were triggered by exposure to onions. But ever so slowly, I began to reconnect to the things that I loved, like cooking, a place where I felt alive again. After a while, it also became a place to consider what I wanted.

Part Two

There's a lot about cooking for one that's just a drag. The leftover thing, prepping, cooking, cleaning up all by yourself, and eating alone. It's all so different now that Phil is gone. One evening I was looking through recipes and came across a delicious-looking dish that called for caramelized onions. It seemed to jump right out of the book. I read the ingredients and immediately laughed.

"Phil would really hate this." I think I said it out loud as I decided to make it.

This recipe called for three pounds of whole yellow onions sliced the French way. Three pounds! Now this was more onions than I'd used on any given day in years. The thought of it, me slicing a pile of onions, just cracked me up. I reached for my most trusted sharpened knife and began carefully doing the French cuts (root and tops off, cut in half, then sliced as evenly as possible into half-moons). They were starting to get to me. I had tears streaming down my face.

I felt Phil right there with me in the kitchen laughing. "Oh, you think this is funny?" I asked, this time for sure out loud.

"Yes, I do," he echoed.

"You and the onions."

I continued laughing and crying and enjoying the aroma of browning onions and melted butter while thinking that I'd missed this particular smell in my kitchen. Apparently, onions and real butter are key ingredients in my recipe for happiness, but strangely, cooking without them for Phil was also. Deep in the black heat of my grandmother's cast-iron skillet was a message for my heart that said, "It's okay for you to stir together your joy and sorrow." Mmm, delicious.

3   tablespoons of unsalted butter
2   tablespoons of olive oil
3   pounds of yellow onions, sliced ⅛ inch thick
     Kosher salt and freshly ground black pepper
1   tablespoon of balsamic vinegar

After slicing the onions, melt the butter and oil and add the onions with a pinch of salt. Sauté for 8–10 minutes over medium-high heat as they soften, reduce heat, and stir as needed until they become a sweet, deep brown, about 45 minutes. Deglaze the pan with red wine or balsamic vinegar.

DRAGONFLY

landed at my breakfast
next to the spoon
Her wings transparent, iridescent...
resting
Was she alive, I wondered?
Had she gotten trapped indoors by an artificial trade wind
swept in on the pull of the door?
What was she doing here
so far from the verdant world
outside the window?
What of her mate and her children?
Her solemn eyes given
to green with flecks of gold
regarded me without interest
I thought for sure she was dead.
I moved in for a postmortem close-up
She shuddered...
allowing one click
and adjusted her banded
blue and green tail.
Definitely not dead.
She turned her triangular face toward me
and fluffed her wings for flight
But not before she
winked one impossibly
large eye.

"My life," she said, "is about
seven of your months.
I intend to live them all.
And you?"
She flew off to other business
and left me to my oatmeal
and wonder.

BREAKFAST WITH BILLIE

Grief is what love sounds like when she's singing the blues.

We agreed to meet at my place; breakfast would be cool, she said. She had a class later in the day.

I made an omelet with fresh herbs from the garden and my famous spicy ginger collard greens. I was slicing roast Peking duck that I bought from my favorite Chinese restaurant when she arrived. I hadn't noticed a knock at the door; she just strolled right in. Billie, looking every bit like jazz royalty even in her coordinated yoga pants.

My dogs didn't stir; they slept peacefully by the door, which was strange as they always make a fuss when somebody new comes over, but I was grateful my honored guest could forgo the usual canine jump-up greeting.

"Is this your place?" she asked, looking around.

"Yes," I answered, suddenly feeling shy.

"Niiice." She drew out the word like smoke from a cigarette. Glancing in the direction of the grand piano, she asked, "You play?"

"Yes," I mumbled. "Well, I'm not really what you'd call . . . I mean, nobody would pay me to play."

"Renting?" She was looking at the group of framed pictures on the bookshelf.

"No," I said. "I mean, I own."

She cut me off. "Good," she intoned in a voice both soft and sure of itself. "Real good. Nobody yelling when the rent is due—threatening to put you out on the street without shoes or shawl." We smiled, nodding in agreement.

"Welcome," I offered. "Have a seat and make yourself at home." Gesturing toward the table, I noticed how gracefully she moved. She looked like a bronze goddess—her skin had an amazing almond glow and her eyes were clear and bright. "You look so good, Ms. Billie," I gushed.

"Thank you," she replied. "I just started taking yoga classes."

—

"Would you like some coffee? I just made a fresh pot." I brought two cups and we settled in at the table facing each other. She was truly a vision. Her face held that kind of beauty that dared you to look away. And her skin was perfect. Damn, she looked good. Better in person than I could have imagined. "Ms. Billie," I said, trying not to stare, "I want to thank you for coming. I hope you're hungry. I made us a fresh herb omelet, some ginger collard greens, and there's some Peking duck too, if you like."

She looked approvingly at the spread before saying, "You know, I've been trying to eat mostly vegetarian. But I might have a taste of that crispy duck. I used to love it, especially the skin." We laughed.

"Try the greens too," I suggested. "I don't use any meat; they're vegan."

"Don't mind if I do." She tasted. "Mmm," she said, smiling. "Now, I don't eat everybody's greens, but these are so good. I'll need that recipe."

We chatted about inventing yourself in a world all set to do it for you. I asked about one of her signature tunes, "Good Morning Heartache," which had recently been playing on repeat in my head. "That song's been around the block a few times since you had a hit with it in the 1940s," I told her. "All the chick singers have covered that song."

"Yeah, I know," she said, looking slightly annoyed.

It was true that singers tried to copy her sound, but they never could quite get it because they didn't have the secret—her secret. "Everybody has their own sound; we're born that way," she insisted. "But somehow, we forget it by trying to copy somebody else. And," she continued, "you can spend a lifetime wasting time, searching for something you already have."

We continued our conversation with talk about being a singer on- and offstage, life on the road, and the ups and downs of what she jokingly called the show-you-the-business. I told her about my husband Phil, his death, our forty-year marriage, three kids, our charmed life, and then I started to cry. "I miss him so much."

"Yeah," she said knowingly. "Of course you miss him. It'd be awful strange if you didn't. Sounds like he was a man worth missing." Smiling, she placed her hand on mine. "There's a difference between missing a real good man who was loyal and kind and missing somebody who was no damn good in the first place. Be sure you distinguish between the two."

She rose and headed back the way she came. The dogs stretched before returning to part two of their morning nap. "I need to hustle; don't want to be late for my yoga class. Thanks for breakfast." She turned, flashing her lovely smile. "You take care of your heart, sugar, okay? And send me your recipe for those collard greens."

A Love Supreme

Thank you, John Coltrane. A song. An album. A path. Thank you for it all. Thank you for the portals opening up in the seen and unseen universes. It was 1964. I was eight years old and had probably heard of New Jersey but couldn't possibly point it out on a map. He was eleven years old, the Phil I had not met yet. He lived in Philadelphia too. Perhaps you saw him at some point? Out of the corner of your eye as you were rushing to a gig? A lanky, light-skinned, tall-for-his-age Black kid. No?

He wouldn't have been hanging out in jazz spots; he was too young for that. And his ears, like mine, were not yet attuned to the sublime call of "A Love Supreme." My young ears had caught wind of the Supremes, the ones hailing from Detroit. In 1964, they asked, "Where did our love go?" And my young Black girl self knew I wanted to *be* a Supreme. I checked the mirror for all that would be necessary to complete this transformation. Skinny legs, check; brown-skinned, check; big eyes, check; wide smile, check. I was shorter by several inches than any of the real Supremes, but chances are I'd grow some, so check. I could sing, too, although my repertoire up to that point consisted of mostly church songs. ("Jesus Loves Me," anyone?)

So I practiced *baby, baby, baby* over and over until it sounded like I knew what I was singing about. But the *hair*, people—the hair, makeup, nails, gowns, all of that! Yes, indeed, I wanted all of that too. Lucky for me, my mother was a hairdresser—a professional one. I might have to wait a few years to persuade her to let me join the Supremes, but it could happen. At this point, it was all I could do to convince my mother to let me wear my hair out, let alone in a skyward-bound beehive style. She styled my hair for the fourth grade in a tight ponytail, braided or cornrowed. Not for the bright stage lights and glamour—the direction in which my imagination pointed.

As it was, I had to sit atop three phone books—the Yellow Pages— in her chair. Once I was raised to a sufficient height, my head leaned back into the bowl, she would wash and rinse. I was usually her last "customer" on Saturday. She was, no doubt, tired from being on her feet all day, so the hairstyles were quick and easy for her, and al- together uninspired from my perspective of supreme stardom.

You, Mr. Coltrane in 1964, you were in New Jersey in the studio creating layers upon layers of a shining path while I was learning to perfect my penmanship. I wanted lovely handwriting, perfect in every way, loop-de-loops in cursive, so I could sign my name on something, like a record contract, just like a grown-up.

Practicing is like reaching for something, something that's just out of reach, a yearning of the spirit, a sprawling query, a curious wanting. You knew about such things, the grasping energy of the spirit. You used the saxophone tool to dig for it, plead and pray, and practice until it could no longer resist you. I'm thanking you now, Mr. Coltrane, for the wonderment of that path that I could neither see nor hear in the 1960s, yet I've felt its placement in the deepest parts of my soul. The love supreme you laid down has guided and sustained me, been a kind of Holy Spirit messenger of creative peace. It brought my beloved lover to my doorstep. Created a space for us to grow in the crucible of marriage—building, searching, designing, through addition and subtraction and teaching us about multiplying, sanctifying, and blending the art of being together on sacred ground. You taught us all about leading with a love supreme. And it became a life habit.

We had no idea at the time, Mr. John Coltrane, no idea at all, that your saxophone, a tool of the spirit, would pave the way for an experience of a lifetime. In the 1960s, if you were a young Black girl, you needed to come to your own rescue through your imagination. I wanted a Barbie doll. I wanted to exercise the imagination of myself on a hard piece of pink plastic and dress her in clothes I fashioned myself. I was cool with the fact that her arms didn't bend. I could pretend that they did, and anyways, this gave her the appearance of always reaching out toward me with a hug of affirmation. I was also cool with the fact that she was blue-eyed and blond—not brown like me.

No matter, I thought, I could play with her and make up adventures where I/she would be the star. I could pretend so hard that no one in my made-up world would notice that she was an immigrant from white imagination. But my mother wasn't having it, not any of it.

"No white dolls," she said. The dolls I already had were handmade from cloth, brown cloth. They had yarn hair and button eyes. But these Raggedy Ann types would never be allowed on my shiny imaginary stage.

"We are learning to appreciate ourselves as Black people," she continued. Try as I might, I couldn't convince my mother that I was strong enough to imagine away white Barbie's whiteness and reform her into a light-skinned version of a Black Barbie. I could even rename her, calling her Denise or Vanessa if that would help, but Mom said, "No," and that was that. There were no Black Barbies for sale in the 1960s, and it would be twenty years before they appeared on toy shelves in small numbers and in select markets. Barbie had Black "friends" (Christie and the like), but it took Mattel a minute to bend the brand and create a bona fide Black Barbie. By then, I was beyond Barbies, having crafted my own little Black girl dreams out of real stuff snatched from *Ebony* magazine and the Supremes, Nina Simone, Nancy Wilson, and Billie Holiday.

"A Love Supreme" was well on its way to our ears and hearts by then, Mr. Coltrane, sailing through the ether in the eighties.

We found each other, my love and I, on a summer porch right around the corner from your birthplace in Hamlet, North Carolina. We knew immediately and recognized the light in each other's eyes. We stopped, souls rejoicing, aware of our great fortune in finding one another again. We double-checked, just to be certain.

What do you like to read and watch?

Answer: *Dune* by Frank Herbert, sci-fi, *Star Trek*.

What music do you listen to?

Answer: Jazz, Coltrane, R & B, James Brown, Earth, Wind & Fire, and funk.

Well, all right then, it *is* you.

And your composed piece "A Love Supreme," a living witness to our connection, was reverberating, sounding itself at that moment. We loved and lived, and made beautiful babies, career moves, and mistakes. We grew and forgave each other and ourselves for times when our love felt less than supreme. And then one day in March 2016, when we were riding high on life, enjoying family and career and thinking about the good old days to come, the refrain uprising in "A Love Supreme" began unraveling, repeating, again and again, its soul message.

The doctor handed Phil, my beloved, a diagnosis. We shook our heads, staring in disbelief. "No," we said, almost in unison. This is not ours. Perhaps we misheard you, what did you say of Phil's diagnosis?

The doctor replied: "Amyotrophic lateral sclerosis . . . ALS."

It was then that you blew your saxophone so loud, Mr. Coltrane! They thought we were in shock, but in reality, we just couldn't believe they couldn't hear you too. The room was literally vibrating with your soul spirit fierceness. How could they not hear? You blew past that damned prognosis, all those little sounds suggesting this or that treatment. You blew past the next appointment, protocols, support groups, experimental drugs, all that. You were playing pure love like our lives depended on it. Hot, stanky, black smoky sheets pouring out that horn of yours.

A LOVE SUPREME!
A LOVE SUPREME!
A LOVE SUPREME!

Thank you, Mr. Coltrane. Thank you!

I never gave much thought to the word *widow*. It rarely entered my mind—well, except for the infamous female spider with the hourglass shape who killed her unfortunate mate after sex. Her bite could kill. But on a normal day? Nope, widow wasn't a go-to thought for me.

The Sanskrit word for widow is *vidhava*, meaning "empty." The ancient tongue conjures the image of a woman draped in sadness and somehow diminished. The idea of being destitute and not completely whole follows the word *widow* like a veil into the English language.

I guess if one believes the statistics (women living longer than men), one might figure the odds were that I might possibly *be* a widow, but I never really gave it much thought.

I've known women who've lost their husbands, of course. In my own family, my maternal grandmother was indeed a widow, but to me, she seemed a robust and happy person, not diminished in the least. A first cousin buried two husbands in tragic, sudden circumstances. Two husbands! And although she was most certainly a widow, I never referred to her in that way, not in word or thought. There was no voice given to that experience—no discussion of what it felt like to walk that path of widowhood.

I remember getting advice from older women about marriage. Things like "Never let the sun set on your anger." Or "Keep a little cookie jar money for yourself." And "Don't tell all you know." These were words of wisdom about keeping your vows, family life, and how to stay happily married. But not a single word about what happens to you when death does part you, and no conversation at all about how to take care of yourself in case you end up being *by yourself*.

Even as Phil's health continued to decline and we could both see the inevitable creeping toward us, I pushed the thoughts of my future self away, telling myself that caring for Phil was a precious plenty to do. In his final months, we had deep conversations about our life and love, our kids and grandkids, and what was most important to him and to me. These are conversations that I treasure.

We discussed the joy of being each other's soulmate, recalling how we met on a friend's porch in July 1978 and the nearly forty-year journey we'd made together. Phil said it'd be okay with him if I married again after he passed on. I laughed it off by saying that he'd loved me enough for ten lifetimes and I had no interest in another lover, husband, or friend. But the truth was that I couldn't bear the thought of who I'd *be* without him. Thoughts of a future self, the woman whose husband had *died*, were placed on a high shelf, and I had no intention of taking a good look.

Looking back, I realize there was so much we both wanted to say that language just couldn't hold. It was simply inexpressible. The struggle with language continues as I wade through the grief storm.

How many times have we all fumbled as we try to find the *right* words? We're constantly searching for *those* words, the ones that reveal our sympathy and empathy. The ones that communicate an understanding of this human connection we all share in life, death, and loss. Time and time again we are left wanting. We feel we're missing some touchstone that goes beyond "I'm so sorry for your loss."

Are there such words that can stand in the gap of sorrow? Perhaps it's asking *way* too much of them. Maybe the comfort we seek resides in realms of music, touch, dance, and poetry. Perhaps ritual is what we need for these unspeakable moments. We could certainly benefit from some new ways to express the deep mystery that grieving stirs up in us all.

On the morning Phil died, I remember feeling a flood of emotions, including relief that his suffering was over. And there was also a kind of numb disbelief. He died at home in the bedroom we shared. Everything in the room *looked* the same, but how could that be? Phil had died. At the same time, I was never more keenly aware of my wifehood. I *am* his wife...not *was* his wife. This thought played on repeat in my head.

As Phil passed from this life, a huge part of who I am shifted. We'd gotten married in 1979 when we were in our early twenties. All of my adult life was shaped by our marriage and family, and, in that present moment, I was sixty-three years old facing the ultimate shape-shifter—death. Phil exhaled his last breath, and I became an unwilling time traveler. I was transported to a strange territory where "we" and "us" became "me." "Is" became "was." Just like that, I was a new arrival in the land of all that used to be. Resistance—that's what I felt. I wasn't having any of that. I wouldn't speak this foreign language. No, not me. I was determined to *be* the wife I'd been to Philip G. Freelon.

There is a legal definition of a widow that I discovered when handling my beloved's estate matters. I wanted to check the box marked married on one of the official forms. I was told that my marriage had officially ended in the eyes of both the law and the Social Security office on July 9, 2019, the day Phil passed.

What? I asked silently, feeling my inner self climbing up on her high horse. (I keep my high horse handy, right in my purse, just for cases like this, when a sister needs to ride.) Who were they to tell me that my forty-year marriage was over? If I want to call myself married, that's my business, dammit!

What are you saying?

What do you mean?

You want me to . . . to check that freaking box that says WIDOW?

No, I will not. No, indeed.

In my imagination, the conversation went something like this:

SOCIAL SECURITY OFFICE PERSON: You've stated that your husband is deceased, yet you've checked the box that says married. Ma'am, is your husband deceased?

ME: Yes, he is.

SS PERSON: Okay, ma'am, date of death?

ME: July 9, 2019.

SS PERSON: Ma'am, let me say I'm sorry for your loss.

ME: *silence*

SS PERSON: So, we'll need to check the box that says "widow." You are the surviving spouse, correct?

ME: The spouse, yes. I am his spouse—his wife.

SS PERSON: You are the widow, umm, surviving spouse, and—

ME: [*cutting her off*] I prefer to check the box that says "married." We were married forty years. That's all of my adult life.

SS PERSON: Well, ma'am...

ME: If I prefer to remain married and check that box, that's my choice, is it not? You have no right to rename me. You don't know me or my particular situation.

SS PERSON: I cannot process this form if you do not click the correct box. I'm sorry, but those are the rules.

ME: Well, the *rules* need to be changed. Let me speak to a supervisor!

It's true what the old folks say: "It ain't what they call you, it's what you answer to."

WIDOW SONG

Must my heart a widow be
A widow's heart is never free
To have and hold my love for thee
Must my heart a widow be

Must I wear this cloak of gray
give myself to yesterday
To the tender breath of memory
Must my heart a widow be

I have two lovers
Each one so fine
one's name is patience
and the other's name is time

Must I tend this hearth alone
Must my heart turn into stone
A love that lives yet cannot be
Must my heart a widow be
Must my heart a widow be
Must my heart a widow be

MOON RIVER

The rumors are apparently true, the ones about your width. Unable to sleep, I looked out my bedroom window and you were there, having stretched your arms in a wide embrace, a seemingly impossible feat for a river like the Eno, the Mississippi, or mighty Amazon.

I sit on your muddy bank and wonder at the dark. Tonight, there is no moon.

Only stars know the truth of it.
The Moon, the one that belongs to the sky,
the one for whom you are named, needs rest.
Her refusal to shine is an act of self-care.

Still I wonder,
in the crossing did you see him?

He would have been hard to miss, even in the darkness.
Tall, handsome

Probably carrying a briefcase
Probably holding blueprints
for a new project, affordable loving.
Probably wearing an impeccably tailored suit.
Probably pictures of his children and grandchildren in his pockets.
Probably listening to someone singing
"Moon River."
Probably smiling: "That's my wife."

THE LIGHT

Love is bending
refracted by
your absence.
No longer
the shortest
distance
between us.
It meanders around
roots and brambles,
branches of desire.
Today I'm gathering
acorns fallen
from your
windy height.
These will be
my supper.
I'm hungry
and they
hold a certain
point of view
where you kissed me
and I stayed that way.
Ever present
in the light
of your
absence.

LOVE COBBLER

My grandmother taught me how to make peach cobbler. She had a lopsided peach tree in her yard. It had been damaged in a snowstorm, and half of the branches on one side bore no fruit. Short and scruffy, it was unremarkable compared to the neighboring maple and oak trees until summertime, when it gave us a sideshow loaded with pale-yellow peaches.

I loved being my grandmother's helper. My job was to pick the peaches that had fallen to the ground, shaking off the dirt and ants. When I complained about the ants, she said, "Ants know a good sweet peach." I was her "little peachy pie," a nickname that filled me up and made me glad.

Her taste-and-feel recipe was my guide. She'd pinch this, taste that. When I asked her how much flour or salt, all she'd show was her cupped hand and say, "Oh, about this much." And out of her oven came peach perfection, not-too-sweet peachy goodness every single time.

Peach Cobbler

It's now July, and the fresh peaches I bought (on sale) have been ripening in a brown paper bag. Outside, the day is humid and it feels too warm, even for July. At the back of my mind, Grief slowly unfurls her sail. We're headed for some tender cove, years ago, when Phil was alive and well. We were in the kitchen; I was slicing peaches while trying to stay ahead of his slice pilfering.

Phil loved my peach cobbler. It was a special dessert that I only made at the height of peach season. In North Carolina, that happens during a few precious weeks between June and late July. Now, Grief is waving a flag back and forth, its red letters spelling JULY. This month holds my birthday and, on the same date, my mother's. It's the month when Phil and I first met and, more recently, *that July* summer morning when he died. It's no wonder my feelings are complicated and layered.

Ah, and lest we forget why I wanted to bake a cobbler in the first place, July is when I first blew a brother's mind with that peach cobbler.

A river runs through it, winding around the sorrow and joy. It reaches all the way back to peachy pie in my grandmother's yard; up and over summer peaches with salty crust topped with ice cream; through the love of baking a dessert that Phil and the kids loved; to this very moment, where I ready my heart to bake a love cobbler with peaches.

I'm wondering about the peaches ripening in the brown paper bag. Are they reciting sugar hymns to each other in the darkness? Is it easy to soften, to yield to sweetness? These are questions for my own heart to ponder. Does grief over time become a sweet fruit that nourishes?

I'm no expert, but it seems like patience would be required to discover the truth of it.

For now, I'm slicing this sweet mess of peaches, adding them to the big yellow bowl. A memory of swatting his hand away in laughter rides alongside love and rich smells of cinnamon and nutmeg.

Nnenna's Peach Cobbler

Song: "Didn't I (Blow Your Mind This Time)"
— THE DELFONICS

Warning: This is not a recipe. I'm just sharing a couple secrets on the road to perfection. I use 8–10 fresh peaches in season, spiced and sweetened to your liking. Forget frozen, canned, or bottled.

I don't peel but it's up to you. Make a double-layer crust like a lasagna. One layer peach filling, and dot all with butter (real buttah); add crust, second layer peach filling. Lattice the top crust. Taste as you go. Peaches in season should be sweet, although it will vary. I like my cobbler peach sweet, not sugar sweet, with a balance of spices and buttery, slightly salty crust.

Now, as far as the crust goes, for years I made it from scratch. But once I discovered high-quality frozen butter pie crusts, it was an easy decision to use two of those instead.

Bake in a slow oven at 325F° and be patient. It will smell done before it is done.

Crust will be golden brown with peachy goodness bubbling through.

JUST YOU

Sweep away my fear
So I fly straight and true
Let the voice within my soul
Sing my love for you
Every breath a sweeter song
A rising melody
Not the music or the tune
Or the candle in this room
Just you . . .
The heart of my life

You're the sea and shore
The candle and the flame
Now and as before
And all that shall remain
Moments come and go
Yet you're here with me
Not the hour or the day
Or these things that pass away
Just you.
The heart of my life

Through space and time
A grand design
It's you, it's always been you

Let the ladder of your love
Reach all the way to me
And live inside your love
In perfect harmony
Not the journey or the road
That matters now to me
Not the dream of buy and sell
Or the stories time can tell
Just you . . .
The heart of my life

ABSENCE

"Good morning, you sleep okay?" It's a silly question perhaps, but I needed to say something that sounded normal. It's nearly dawn and my clothesline sways in sorrow's tropical breeze. Getting up, I reluctantly prepare to hang another day. Though weary of this ritual, I reach inside the faded bag, rifling through bones of old clothespins for an agreeable one, just one pin, unclenched from the idea of gone.

At this part, my lips tighten, my heart does that skipping thing (a trick recently learned), and I shake my head from side to side, gesturing *no*. Once again, there's no pin unsullied by some version of your departure. With no good alternatives, I'm left with another day to be hung in the presence of your absence.

"What's on your schedule today, honey?" Here's another question meant to provide some starch to the idea of gone, which now hangs on the line but only loosely. I find myself reflecting on various occasions when I've used the word *gone* to answer certain questions.

You were running errands.

You were fishing down at the lake.

You'd left the office, calling to say you'd be home in ten or fifteen minutes.

But this gone was of another sort entirely; it was a stranger who'd come for a visit and decided without permission to stay.

This gone brought her paintbrushes.

Her somber hues.

Her blank canvas.

"Shall we?" she asked.

"Shall we what?" I replied, annoyed at so forward a question from an idea with whom I'd only recently become acquainted.

"Why, paint, of course." She gestured toward an easel at the far corner of my mind.

I glanced there, thinking, "These are not my favorite colors. They're nonspecific, muddy. I want sweet tangerine daylight, the cornflower-blue shade of ever-brightening skies. I reject this persistent misrepresentation of loss. Give me pure, hopeful hues, unpigmented with absence. How is it possible to create anything beautiful on this impoverished canvas?"

"It's almost dinnertime. Want me to cook or shall I make reservations?" It occurred to me that I was beginning to lose touch. There are so many ways to lose touch with people you love. There's an awful subterranean forgetting, where your edge and the edge of all you've known drift further and further apart until even the seeds of language disappear. Maybe my kind of losing it is not *that* kind. Maybe it's a benign sort of thing. My choosing to hold on to you and let the rest of what *gone* means, or could mean, evaporate.

———

Perhaps I can, by spinning gossamer threads of denial, somehow weave them into rope sturdy enough to become a tether. Maybe it'd be even stronger than memory and could replace the clothesline currently in use, the one that's been sagging under the weighty days of your absence.

JUST SWEET ENOUGH

Grief knows your entire name. The one written on your birth certificate and the nickname that only your mama calls you. She's way too familiar with intimate details, like the way your beloved said your name so that it hung in the air, a suspended invitation. Yes, she has her own particular way with you because she's made you into a habit.

Like a second skin slipping inside your emotional cracks and crevices, watching, waiting: You hardly notice her quiet approach, that wisp of nothing. After all, you're just living your life, right? Little do you know that a keen observer has been snooping all the while. That's how she knows all your ins and outs. Those inner conversations that maybe even you were unaware of? Grief's totally been taking notes. She's an eavesdropper, that Grief; nothing is hidden, nothing is sacred.

There are, of course, obvious places where Grief appears as her natural self. We are accustomed to seeing her at the funeral. We feel her moving among us, pressing our hearts with ungentle hands. And at the bedside of a dying loved one when goodbye feels like more than you can bear, she's right there, an expected if unwelcome presence. We like to think we can mark those customary life places where she's apt to make an appearance, but with Grief it's never that simple.

I'm learning not to underestimate Grief's potential to show up when you least expect her. In the guise of the absolutely ordinary, she wanders in and triggers an emotional avalanche. I've been hit more than once—toppled head over heels without a moment's notice—while cooking, folding clothes, walking the dog, and braiding my hair.

Like the constant drip, drip, drip of a leaky faucet, Grief is a stain maker, marking those places you hadn't thought about in years, places you thought were insignificant. Grief throws them into sharp relief, evidence that she can go wherever you have been. And so it was with a simple bowl of oatmeal. My appetite was one of the first things that changed in my grieving body. I had little desire to eat right after Phil passed. Everything tasted flat—no flavor, no joy. Food had always been my language of love, and cooking for Phil and our family was a place where I felt love and shared my joy. For me the kitchen was like being onstage.

Meals were shared and enjoyed together. I was happiest in the gathering 'round the family table. Even after the kids left the nest, Phil and I looked forward to weekly family dinners and my experimental recipes. In the early month's shadow of his departure, the joy I had known in this area of my life shifted. Breakfast, lunch, and dinner, along with the prep, cooking, and clean-up, became one more sorrowful burden. Cooking for one? Eating alone? No, thank you.

Of all the meals, breakfast seemed to carry the most emotional weight. The sun would rise on my sleepless night and I'd meet that hard truth once again: My husband Phil had died. Hard, hard truth.

I think I survived on coffee and toast for most of the days and weeks following Phil's departure. Until one morning about three months after he died—I woke up starving. It struck me as weird since the growling of my stomach had been quiet. It was sort of nice to consider "What do I feel like eating this morning?" During Phil's illness I prepared "kitchen sink" smoothies filled with fruits, coconut oil, and supplements said to be good for those with ALS. This was the breakfast of champions, he used to joke. While they were not absolutely delicious, we both drank them in hopes it would do some good. Although I had a stockpile of smoothie ingredients, I definitely didn't want one that morning. Nor did I feel like a big ol' Southern biscuit breakfast with grits, eggs, and such like we used to enjoy on the weekends. After so much time avoiding breakfast altogether, I didn't want to launch an aerial assault on my tummy.

Then I had an epiphany. Oatmeal, I thought, would be perfect. Filling, healthy, and, best of all, I knew I had some on the third shelf of the cupboard. Oatmeal it is! I reached up to grab the cylindrical box with the familiar image of the man in the blue hat with a kindly face and smiling eyes, and I just froze, suddenly overcome with profound sadness. There was something in the atmosphere, some great resistance calling me to attention. I had no choice but to sit still and listen to the oatmeal's story. I sat down, oatmeal box in hand, as a conversation began to unravel in my mind. Mind you, all this transpired before my coffee, so I was in a very vulnerable state.

It was our morning breakfast ritual playing like an old soul record, except Grief had placed the needle down on this very ordinary oatmeal story.

ME: Phil, what do you want for breakfast?

PHIL: I'll have oatmeal, honey.

ME: Oatmeal. Okay.

PHIL: Yes, let's have oatmeal.

ME: Okay. [*Reaching in the cupboard*] Regular Quaker Oats or steel cut?

PHIL: Ah, let's do steel cut.

ME: Now you know steel-cut oats take thirty minutes to cook.

PHIL: Yeah, I know. I'm good. Steel cut.

I begin by adding the steel-cut oats to the boiling water. Stirring, I have one eye on the boiling pot, one eye on Phil trying to make coffee. He's checking his emails or reading something, and I'm just enjoying these morning moments with a dim realization that there may be fewer mornings like this in our future.

Then, I ask Phil, as if I didn't know:

ME: What do you want in it? In your oatmeal?

PHIL: We got any bananas?

ME: Hmm, yes, we have some bananas. A few are a bit ripe, but I think we can make it work.

I was hoping the bananas weren't the type that tended toward lies. Those with smooth yellow skin but mushy inside. Phil disliked "banana bread bananas," unless they were actually in banana bread, of course.

PHIL: Do we have walnuts or pecans?

ME: Lemme check. [*I go to the pantry and see that we have both.*] Yes, we have both.

PHIL: Okay, I'll have both.

ME: Okay, both.

We both smile a knowing smile.

PHIL: Aaand, do we have any craisins?

ME: We don't. Umm, we do have raisins, though. You want raisins?

PHIL: No, I don't want raisins.

I search around and find some dried cherries.

ME: Phil, you want dried cherries?

PHIL: Yes, please. I'll have a few dried cherries.

ME: Cinnamon?

PHIL: Yes, yes, please.

ME: You want honey or brown sugar?

PHIL: I think it's gonna be sweet enough.

This back-and-forth conversation was a mundane, beautiful slice of our lives. It's not as if after almost forty years I didn't *know* that he liked all possible options in his oatmeal—and in life. That if I offered walnuts or pecans he'd always say, "Gimme a little of both." 'Cause that's the kind of guy he was. That he liked cinnamon on top and non-mushy bananas and didn't care for raisins. Honey, maple syrup, and brown sugar weren't necessary for him to enjoy the sweetness of the moment.

Grief met me right at the bowl. Smack-dab in the middle of an ordinary moment made extraordinary in the wake of my beloved's passing. While the loving offering of breakfast together had changed forever, I was also reminded that very ordinary moments were sweet enough to sustain me—if I could just let them.

OATMEAL

I haven't had a bowl since you
passed.
Our fragrant morning
ritual of almond milk
nuts and craisins
seemed too
much to bear.
There have been at least
100 breakfasts since then.
Each deliberately steering toward
dry toast or
things *not* oatmeal.
This morning, I offer prayer
as I add water
to cast iron
add oats steel cut
to the
roiling maelstrom.
Prayer that you will
meet me in our kitchen
at this joyous bowl.
This cinnamon
altar.

THE DISHWASHER

Grief delivers large and small losses. Familiar patterns and old habits are places where I've felt the most unexpected heartache. My husband, Phil, was a handyman's handyman. He rarely called a repair person. He never read the owner's manual or instructions. He'd investigate the broken thing, figure out the problem, dive in, and fix it, period.

When our kids were little, they'd bring their broken toys to their father. And he'd say, "And Dad can fix ... ?" The kids knew their line by heart. "Just about anything!" they'd squeal with delight. And this was absolutely true—and somewhat of a miracle to me as a person with zero mechanical skill. Early in our marriage I'd sit by him and carefully read the instructions. "It says here to attach B to C using an Allen wrench," I'd say. He'd give me one of his big eyebrow looks that meant "I got this." And he did.

Perhaps because Phil had such a hard time with reading when he was young, he taught himself the awesome powers of observation and listening. He was able to see how things were engineered to work together. He was a model builder, a puzzle solver, and a design thinker. Once I asked, "How can you fix something you've never even seen before?" I will never forget his answer. Phil said, "The person who made this is no smarter than I am."

Wow. I had to sit with that for quite a while, realizing that whenever I encountered a technical situation or a set of assembly instructions, I said to myself, "I can't do this," and it became my truth. But for Phil, this problem never existed. Even when ALS made it impossible for Phil to hold a tool or bend down and look to see what the issue was, we devised a plan. I'd use my phone to snap a picture of the problem, no matter if it was an error code or a kink in the drainpipe, and send it to him. He'd instruct me to get the pliers or wrench or whatever was needed and lead me step by step. Sometimes I didn't know the difference between a needle-nose and a hex nut, but I'd take a pic and he'd say yes or no and we were off to the races. We used teamwork and technology to move through those challenges. I really loved those moments when we collaborated in the fix-it world. I didn't even want to think about who would fix things once Phil was gone.

One morning, I awoke to a dishwasher full of half-cleaned dishes and dirty water. My first thought was *Phil would know just what to do.* At that moment, I felt a new pang of loss on top of a stinky dishwasher that needed fixing. I called a repair company, hoping to get someone out later that day. After several phone calls to different companies, the first available appointment was more than a week out. I sat down, lamenting my situation, when I heard Phil's voice echoing in my ears: "The person who made this is no smarter than you are."

True, the person wasn't smarter, but what I didn't know about dishwashers could make a whole new world. The thought of not having a working dishwasher for a week, though, motivated me to do something, along with the memory of Phil's words.

I searched "error code 24," which meant there was a blocked drain hose. Inside the dishwasher I saw smooth steel from top to bottom, not a hose in sight. The person who made this machine was definitely smarter, or at least more hose-savvy. Frustrated, I decided to take a break. Taking a break helps. I searched YouTube for a video with a simple answer to my problem. After about an hour and scrolling through lots of ads for repair hoses, I found a video that was fairly easy to understand. The instructions involved bailing out dirty water, removing the cover from the drain, scooping out a surprising amount of organic food material, replacing everything, and then running a complete cycle. As I followed the video step by step, I had high hopes of being crowned fix-it queen.

But when I opened the door, to my great disappointment, the dishwasher was half filled with warm, gray water. My YouTube efforts had failed. I cried a few tears at that point. Phil used to fix things, and now he was gone and nobody could help until next week. I decided to at least bail the water again and resolved to call the repair company to make an appointment. After that, I closed the door, and something said, "Get the flashlight."

It was Phil's voice, and I've learned to pay attention when I hear him speak in my spirit. The flashlight? Really? I'd already cleared every grain of rice and slimy corn kernel. There wasn't anything blocking anything else; the pump must be broken or something.

Again I felt or heard, "Get the flashlight." So I reluctantly got the flashlight. On hands and knees, I aimed it at the plastic filter. I loosened it to inspect it again. Nothing. It was all clear...except for something shiny reflecting the light. I reached in a bit further to find a small piece of broken glass wedged inside the drain. I removed it with my gloved hand and just sat there, awestruck and happy.

I knew this was my Phil helping me. It was a huge victory for my heart. We are still connected in ways that defy logic. And I didn't need to understand. It was enough to know that he could still fix just about anything.

BLUE SKIES

Clouds
drift.
Thumbprints
pressed on these particular
blues.
And you
have
become
the weather.
The narrow
listing
sense of time
forecasts
anguish
joy
and perhaps
both.
The windsock
whistles a
familiar
melody.
"Blue Skies"?
I've never
heard
it sung
in
this register.

"These Stories We Hold" is a song I co-wrote and recorded in 1996 with Bill Anschell. I had no idea at the time what an important role storytelling would play in my life. Stories have been a lifeline for me on my grief journey. There were times when the threads of memory and story, both real and imagined, were all that held my fragile heart together. Grief had amplified the storytelling voices in my head. Many of these were scary, focused on what-ifs and disaster scenarios. I struggled to shake loose dark thoughts, but they returned with a vengeance, sometimes disguised as thoughts of common sense and caution. After a while, a pattern emerged—first a disaster story of some sort and then my response, complete with plans to avoid it.

This is part of the reason grieving left me so exhausted. There was a whole lot going on most of the time. I found that one way to navigate in the vacuum of grief was to create stories that lifted my spirit. I'd always kept a journal. Writing down my thoughts and dreams was a way of keeping it real with myself. The umbilical cord linking song and story had always been present, but after my recent losses, the connections seemed to become more amplified. Maybe it was the timbre of mourning, but I was drawn to the interstitial spaces between lyric and melody. I longed to stretch words' capacity to reach the grieving heart. Improvising with call-and-response, repetition, rhythm, hums, and whispers eventually found its way into my storytelling podcast, *Great Grief*. And more than ever, I was grateful for this improvisational practice.

In search of our Mother's Garden / We have come to find / Intimate connection of heart and mind

Stories unearthed and exposed by the dissonant tones of loss; the voices of my mother and grandmother literally speaking to me in the mother tongue.

Struggle and triumph herstory told / Lessons of living unfold

Old half-forgotten tales my parents used to tell about growing up down South, stories about the difference between not having a lot of things and being poor.

Her song of survival rising like prayer / These are the gifts that she bears

New narratives of a reimagined life, sorrow and love song, folk-tales, bedtime stories—they all collided in a world colored by grief and charged by improvisation. Engaging with my profound losses helped me feel less afraid. I mean, the worst had already happened. My beloved soulmate had left the planet and my only sister—my running buddy and bestie too. This sorrow was unmatched by anything I'd experienced before, but having accompanied them both on their journey, I felt less afraid of my own death.

Wintertime has turned her garden's / Harvest into gold

I was neither strong nor brave enough to withstand the heavy weight of sorrow. Pretending, ignoring, or doing both at the same time was impossible. If I was to survive at all, I needed permission to be my authentic self, grief-charged, and this had to be okay on- and offstage. Performing a soft-shoe of "I'm doing fine" even for seventy-five minutes felt like another kind of mourning.

Who knew I'd need the tools developed as a jazz musician to select new keys to suit my heart? *Who are you? Where is your story?* I can still hear my mentors Dr. Billy Taylor, Jeri Brown, Sheila Jordan, and Dr. Yusef Lateef in different ways and by individual example ask me to probe my heart for answers. And it's an essential ask.

How do you show up in your art?

In what ways does your story inform your choices? Fill your cup?

It soon becomes clear, the differences between art: authentic versus the onstage act—polished, buffed, and ready for consumption.

This is our treasure / Stories, stories we hold.

I'm learning to love the broken beauty of my instrument and not judge it. Period. I'm singing new songs in the dark to a dawn I can't quite visualize. Grief has permitted me to explore what lies beneath the skin of sorrow. Private, vulnerable stories bubbled to the surface asking to be seen and heard.

Lift my voice and sing? Share my particular stories? Really?

"Yes" was the answer. "Dig where your tears fall."

THESE STORIES WE HOLD

In search of our Mother's Garden
We have come to find
Intimate connection of heart and mind
Struggle and triumph herstory told
Lessons of living unfold

Her song of survival rising like prayer
These are the gifts that she bears

Wintertime has turned her garden's
harvest into gold
This is our treasure
Stories, stories we hold.

UPRISING

There are things that live below the surface. They have their own ways about them and, although unseen, do exist. Feelings are like this, bubbling and churning underneath the skin of life, and grief most certainly shares these characteristics.

Smooth and glasslike, the surface of the lake outside my back door tells me that all is calm. It's greenish brown. It's impossible to guess at the depth, but I've been told by my neighbors that it's fifteen to twenty-five feet deep at least. I've seen folk swim in the pond, and their splashing laughter leads me to believe this is fun being had.

I walk the lake's edge picking up yards of twisted fishing line, rusty cans, and discarded bits of cellophane, thinking, *Maybe I could stick my toes in*. But I don't. The lake's edge is a fine and proper distance for me.

All nine turtles on a half-submerged log slide in as I approach. One by one they all but disappear, save for those little green heads bobbing up and down. Hmm, turtles don't bite, do they?

I feel a song coming through, something about turtles, easy slip-page, swimming, and what lies beneath the surface. It's hazy, this songlet, just a vague notion of story—no melody. Inspiration is fickle. Sometimes you receive a complete download: melody, storyline, rhyme scheme, and rhythm. If you're able to catch the drift before it dissipates, you feel like you've captured a pirate's ransom. Other times, you cast your line in the direction of favorable winds and wait. Sometimes this waiting is rewarded with a half thought, or it could be nothing but vapor. Dangling magic just out of your reach, Grief can tempt you into believing it will always be this way. I'm getting a strong feeling about the turtle song. I walk back to the house humming a slice of melody and thinking of words besides *crepe myrtle* that rhyme.

APPLAUSE

"Open your hands," she said.
I wondered how she could ask such a thing of me
considering what we both knew I'd been through.
She repeated in a kinder, more loving way.
I looked at my hands, which were no longer hands.
They'd been gentle, caressing once.
They'd soothed and stroked, lifted,
wiped, and washed.
They'd pushed themselves
into pyramids of praying faith.
They'd waved goodbye.
And now, they'd become furious fists.
Fingernails had grown teeth. Hanging on
to absence, which is to say nothing.
"Open," she said once more,
  pointing to the
  clenched balls on my lap.
"I want to give you something," she went on.
"These balls are very good for punching, pounding,
  but they were not designed to receive gifts."
"Open is not easy," I cried.
"Neither is closed." She smiled.
She left me to wonder
if my long-curled palms
had forgotten offerings of
applause.

LOVING-KINDNESS

Your acts of kindness are iridescent wings of divine love, which linger and continue to uplift others long after your sharing. — RUMI

There's been much written on kindness. Ancient philosophers, poets, psychologists, and even evolutionary biologists have written on the importance of it, even if they don't exactly agree on why this is so. The Bible, the Koran, and other great religious texts have a lot to say about loving-kindness.

I was taught that living a kind and virtuous life was a gateway into paradise, where rewards waited for the chosen few. I pray that this is true. That in the sweet by-and-by, the great decision-maker will find I've been kind enough. Lately, in the hailstorm of grief, I'm noticing the power of kindness in other ways. I received a flood of cards and letters in the weeks and months following Phil's death. Some were from family, others from friends and colleagues who beautifully expressed the ways in which Phil's life had impacted theirs. And in every single one of them, a story about his kindness.

President Barack Obama and First Lady Michelle Obama sent a heartfelt letter to our family that spoke in detail of Phil's impact personally and professionally through his design leadership as architect of record of the Smithsonian Museum of African American History and Culture. There were personal reflections of his steadfast kindness when it might have felt easier not to be. I was moved that people from all walks of life took the time to write that Phil's life truly mattered and that they would miss him and his kindness.

One letter was from a stranger. Her letter had gone to our previous address, and then it was kindly forwarded. It had been months since Phil died, and the cards, letters, and expressions of love had slowed to a trickle. Yet this letter arrived in divine order, on a day when my heart needed some gentleness. The letter was from a mother whose son had a talent for drawing and an interest in architecture. He was a bright young Black man, an average middle school student who had never met an architect, let alone one of color. She had written a letter to Phil years ago, asking if he'd be willing to send a note to her son. Phil reached out to the mother, inviting them both to visit the Freelon Group office. After giving them a tour and introducing them to some of the young Black architects in his employ, Phil reviewed the young man's drawings, which were quite good. He spent an afternoon sharing encouraging words about the arts, the architectural profession, and life. That encounter had happened several years ago, reported the mother. Her son was now a first-year student at North Carolina A&T University, and he was interested in pursuing architecture. She ended her letter to me with condolences on Phil's passing and with gratitude for his kindness to a complete stranger and her child on that day so long ago.

This letter was a gift to my soul. It was a revelation that one could actually live inside someone else's kindness. And that such kindness could bear a thousand beautiful fruits from trees that you neither planted nor knew existed.

My entire body is my instrument. When I sing, the pulse of melody and words; fluctuations in vibrato; the layered colors of timbre, tone, and silence rise within. Singing requires all of me, head to toe. Music rides on my breath, and when it's flowing, much of it lies in a subtle space beneath my conscious mind. These days, I'm learning that grief is a whole-body experience too.

"Silence is that mysterious place from which everything emanates and eventually returns to." I wrote this in a journal years ago. Reading these words now in consideration of my grief is weird. I could not have possibly understood the gravity and multiple meanings when I wrote those words in the late eighties. Stumbling upon them in this season feels like a message in a bottle. Is Phil letting me know that he, too, has returned to that silent place?

In some ways, silence felt very scary. I was afraid that life as a singer would be impossible with a voice literally torn at the seams. Before I beheld the full face of Grief, I enjoyed a freedom of expression relatively unencumbered by loss. No sad songs for this sister; give me an up-tempo happy blues if you please.

But in this present moment, I was being asked to love fully my utterly broken life. What I really wanted was my previous life back, to reenter its sense of wholeness and the voice that went with it.

Sorrow had me counting up losses, and my career seemed destined for that list. In my solitude, there was quite a bit of Grief's whispered pestering.

GRIEF: Hey there, you feel like singing with me?

ME: No... Thank you.

GRIEF: Why not?

ME: Because, it's obvious. I can't. I'm afraid I won't sound like I used to.

GRIEF: No need to be afraid that you won't sound like you used to. I guarantee you won't.

ME: Thanks a lot. [*Weary sigh*]

GRIEF: So, you singing with me or what?

Grief kept calling on me to sing a new song with her and to breathe deep in sorrow's darkness. I sat firmly in my resistance, unwilling to take the risk that my voice would sound as broken as my heart. I was afraid to bear witness to it. There were only two realities—a *before* and an *after* me. It never entered my mind there might be a third or perhaps an infinite number of alternate realities.

Exhausted from clenching my heart and jaw, I refused my usual vocal rituals. Warm-ups and vocal exercises seemed pointless given my current state. Practice used to be the place where I encountered inspiration. I loved playing with phrasing and tempo, changing the key to see what new personalities emerged, but my life had changed—I'd changed. My desire and wonder evaporated. Books I'd read on grief suggested that this was all very normal, that in due time, life would establish an equilibrium. But that was just it. Grief had me living outside of time. My losses ushered in a temporal shift, and I stumbled around like a ghost, wearing the skin of someone I used to be.

GRIEF: Why do you compare your singing to the former versions?

ME: Because I was happy with those versions.

GRIEF: You've changed, you know.

ME: Yes, I know. I'm broken now.

GRIEF: And your point is?

During months of hushed and exaggerated silence, the scales slowly began to tip and my resistance became much more uncomfortable than my curiosity. I mourned the lost singer in my soul. I yearned to sing yet wasn't prepared to meet my own grief onstage, in front of an audience. I also didn't have the energy to pretend I was fine while singing to a roomful of strangers.

Here's where Grief taught me a profound lesson. I had to learn to trust my authentic self, on- and offstage. It was that simple. Either I could offer myself a bit of grace, or not sing at all. I realized my biggest fear was rooted in self-judgment.

Singing on the breath of my truth, I simultaneously practiced self-care and offered love and respect for all that it means to be an artist, a Black woman—a vulnerable, imperfect human and, most of all, a worthy one. The part about worthiness was huge. I had to ask myself, "Am I worthy of self-love and care?" I realized that being strong (or appearing that way) had mattered more than my being authentic and real.

Stepping out on faith, I discovered a freedom of expression that reached far beyond my expectations. And the universe seemed to grant all kinds of permission that extended beyond the realm of performance. The audience and I crossed over to intimate places of joy and sorrow.

What a revelation to feel this extraordinary depth of human connection in a place where I never expected to find it.

THE ALTAR

In church, the altar call was the point when the music, warm and welcoming, bade you come up in front of everyone to accept Jesus Christ as your Lord and Savior. I'd try to shrink as small as possible while the preacher was saying something like "If anyone is ready to be saved—to give their soul to the Lord—come to the altar!"

I always thought he knew by peering into my eyes that my soul was in particular need of saving. Nodding, I'd try to mirror the expressions of those who looked as if they knew the risks that accompanied refusing this opportunity. If no one felt ready for saving at the moment, the preacher would go on, asking those needing prayer to step up. There were always plenty of folks in need. Both the saved and unsaved kneeled with their heads bent and eyes closed.

An altar is a place of transformation in both real and figurative senses. I stood at that same altar with Phil in 1979 and answered "I do" to a question that I didn't truly understand at the time. Whew, I wonder how many folks would promise "until death do us part" if they knew what it could mean. As I've grown older, the altar has become less of a fine table in a church building or a symbolic place of sacrifice. Now, the altar is where I seek communion with spirit.

I've created an altar in my home to honor and remember Phil. It helps me remember our lives together. From time to time, I change the items assembled on the table and refresh them with crystals, photos, and the gift of a hawk feather, which makes it feel alive with spirit.

Walking in nature, especially near water, feels like the coming forth of an altar—as I take in the birds, the trees, crawling, buzzing creatures, the breeze, and sometimes the rain. Their prayers were far more eloquent than most have heard in a sanctuary. And on any given day, the message was always attuned to my heart's needs.

Recently, I began cooking with more gratitude and reverence. I was trying to be gentle with (but not sorry for) myself as I prepared meals. And I noticed that offering gratitude while peeling the carrots or washing the greens slowed me down, allowing an invitation to unfold. In this way, making dinner became something more than it was. Giving myself permission to imagine cooking for one as an approach to the altar changed how I was feeling. As an offering, the act of meal preparation itself felt sacred. Gratitude became a kind of nourishment poured into the empty bowl, the vacant place setting.

Grief vision is a real thing and a new practice for my heart. I'm not sure I'd be looking for altars to show up while working in the garden, when waiting in line at the post office, or in a stranger's smile, but the altar awaits in the face of the everyday.

I call softly to her from across the fence of time. Every day the space between us lengthens. It seems to me that we should at least remain acquainted, if not cordial. After all, we are his lovers, both of us, in different ways for sure, but lovers just the same. I shift my weight from one foot to the other, wanting to sound more casual than I feel. "I miss him" is all I can utter. She looks directly at me, her gaze unreadable, touching me everywhere. I clear my throat, suddenly feeling like I'm at an audition. She looks past my false cool and doesn't smile.

Can she detect the hiss of sorrow behind my fancy mask?

I've tried to leave these histories alone and wonder if it's wrong to stir things up again.

But we have unfinished business.

I think of her rising on tiptoe to meet his kiss, and of his body curling around hers like a dark ribbon. Recalling their laughter at the punch line to his jokes brings a bittersweet smile. He truly loved her and, more than that, her imperfections—the ways they fit so neatly within his own.

A silvery hum rises in the air between us. Is she going to sing? Will she extend an invitation to me to blend in harmony? Her soprano holds the fragrance of honey, bright and clear, shimmering with hope and blue skies. It bears some of the staining of loss—How could it not?—but the timbre; it's experience, a study in joy-filled living. I nervously whisk a nonexistent fiber from my face, noting the differences between our voices. My voice, reshaped on the whetstone of grief, bears its breaking loosely, as if holding too tightly would cause it to shatter. There's a loving ache in my tone, not golden like hers but burnished with the colors of longing and loss.

~

She's wearing a blouse that I haven't seen for the longest time. He loves that color on me. I was sure I'd donated it to Goodwill, but who can remember one light-blue blouse in the storm of so many things tossed away? She notices my left hand. My wedding rings sparkle. "Oh, I just cleaned them," I mention. She nods, knowing full well that we're still married, but not like they were, of course. Ours is an altogether different affair. They had a forty-year relationship, three kids, and seven grandkids when he passed away in 2019. Yes, I know the whole story.

I also know that it was she and not me who held his hands and heart as they trudged through his illness. She alone wept in secret, not wanting him to know how much it hurt to witness the toll on his body and spirit. Her love for him never wavered. She kept her promises to love and cherish.

In his final hours, he invited me to sit with her. He'd tried so many times before to speak of me, to let her know about me, to offer her some comfort in the knowledge of our special love. But there was so little time in the end.

He was reaching for us both, I'm sure of it, as he whispered a final "I love you." As the light slowly faded from his eyes, from the bedroom, the world, she turned toward me, unable at that moment to meet my eyes. And then, only a beautiful sound echoed as she left.

It's been four years since then. I don't know how long it's been for her, since her temporal reality differs from mine. I'm still getting used to a spiritual love affair. It's true that I get to love him for the rest of my life. But what I wouldn't give to hear the sound of his voice, to feel his touch, his laughter. Sometimes, I listen to voicemail just to hear him, those tiny speakers a bridge to another world.

On the radio an alto saxophone is playing "Over the Rainbow." The lyrics float in lazy circles inside my head. *Somewhere.* I wonder if he's way up high in that land. Every night I climb the ladder, hoping to catch a glimpse of him. I've been wishing upon a star, praying to the moon, but can't seem to awaken from this crazy dream that he's not here—at least not like he used to be.

She had another life with him, a beautiful branching love that blossomed over the years like a rose. I watch her from my side of the fence. She looks younger; her eyes, although sad, are softer than mine. No translucent ghosts shift in her peripheral vision.

—

As she begins to turn away, something in me unravels and I reach out, taking her sad, lovely face in my hands. Kissing her on both cheeks, I whisper, "It's okay."

Time Traveler

FOURTH MOVEMENT

TIME TRAVELER

Music carves a place on the outskirts of time.

Spring is unfolding herself. In my yard, flowers are early announcers: "Breaking News!" and "This Just In: Daffodils! Purple Crocus Have Arrived!" They are being totally themselves, and I'm trying to be a good student of the truth of it.

I watch the new birds arrive after winter's slow exit. They carry an ancient understanding of how to move as the days grow longer. Sensing the coming forth of new life, they follow the urge to head south or north. No one *tells* them. This knowledge is part of belonging.

I think I can feel it tugging on me too. A notion to burst forth and birth newness. Something is keeping me up at night. *Something* is creating discomfort, bidding me to wake up! Sleep later! There's much to do, taste, and feel.

My podcast, *Great Grief*, and my recording *Time Traveler* have been on my heart and mind. Both projects required that I stretch in new ways. Those of us who practice yoga are familiar with the sensation when you reach beyond your edge of comfort.

Some nights, I just lie there trying to find the trail of sleep, asking my busy brain to quiet itself. Other times I sit up and record musings into my phone. Often it's as mundane as a to-do list. I read somewhere that if you list the things that are on your mind, you can then go peacefully back to dreamland. So far no good, for me at least.

One night the moon was so bright that in my half-awake state I thought it was almost dawn. I opened my eyes and the moon seemed to fill up the whole night sky. She was literally in bed with me, her beams lighting the covers.

Moonspeak is different from suntalk. The moon hums and whispers your name. She knows how to get your inner attention. And from the edge of your awareness, she'll share her secrets if you listen.

On this particular night, she was in her fullness and especially talkative. She half-whispered, "Your new recording is called... *Time Traveler*?"

"Yes," I said, wondering how she knew.

"How lovely," she sighed. "I'm a time traveler too. Tonight I traveled over 238,000 miles just to be with you."

I was too astonished to speak.

"I'll tell you a secret," she whispered. "Do you remember when you were little and you told your big brother that the moon was following you?"

"Yes," I replied. "And I also remember him laughing at me and saying that the moon follows everybody."

"Well, here's the thing," she said in a very lunary way, "I, the moon, may *appear* to follow everybody but I actually do follow certain people like you. Time travelers, we call them."

"Time travelers?" I said, "Well, it's the name of my new CD, but—"

"Ah, yes," she interrupted. "And it's also *who you are*. You make music and it makes you. Music, my dear, is energy, and well..." She continued, laughing, "I'm over four billion years old, and believe me, I've seen a thing or two."

"But how, I mean, what?" I couldn't finish my thought. Does the moon have a sense of humor?

She continued, "It's your music, my love. Music bends time.

"You know how a song can take up residence in your heart and play itself over and over? Or have you wondered how it's possible that a melody can take you right back to a place you recall as the past? Well, as far as music is concerned, the past, present, and future overlap. They're all quite the same thing. It's magic," she said, giggling. "This energy, this music is the first language," she shared.

"You were worrying tonight, so I thought I'd pay you a visit to let you know it's fine," she said softly. "We're time travelers, you and I, that's all. Go to sleep now."

END OF THE GARDEN

It's late summer. My garden is finished. Everything is bending toward the ground except for the tall stand of okra bearing a few huge, inedible pods. I've decided to gift them to the birds. I recall a tune I used to love by Dakota Staton called "The Late, Late Show." It was a swinging number, her voice on the hook a playful tease: "We're putting on the late, late show!"

My garden is doing its own somber version of the late, late show. I wade among the twisted vines and drying stalks, all that's left from the summer bounty of peppers, eggplant, cucumbers, and herbs, while trying to decide if I have enough energy to pull the dead plants, turn the soil, and mulch. This activity presumes another planting, a future dance of growth and hope. At this moment, I don't feel particularly full of hope or anything else. I feel empty. My garden seems like a reflecting pool for my beating heart.

It's over now, over now, over now.

"It's too hot," I think. "This can wait until later. Much later." I brush past a tangled forest of draped brown leaves—a final embrace. I bend my head and shoulders down to assess if this chore and my energy are a good match when I notice a familiar slender dark purple that's half hidden. An eggplant? Hello! How did I miss you? Not big enough for a meal, but still. Encouraged by my meager find, I continue the search among the crisping leaves and find, to my surprise, seven more Ichiban eggplants. Now this, I think, has the makings of a possible dinner, and further inspection reveals a small bell pepper having lingered for so long that it turned bright red, three shishito peppers, and a huge jalapeño streaked with yellow. I am surprised and humbled by these final gifts from my garden, which I'd thought was at an end.

Just because it's all I had, it's what I made. The ingredients for a late-summer supper were a generous gift and an ode to an improvisational moment composed of time and truth. As I sliced them, I gave thanks for these plants that lasted through a dry summer. And it occurred to me that my thirsty heart had also braved the summer heat of sorrow. Thank you, teacher garden, for a bit of love's nourishment when I was seemingly at the end of things.

THE CELEBRANT

My grief journey has often taken me to a place that feels just like a fictional story. My love of science fiction is part of what drew me to Phil and informs my view of what's possible.

The suspension of belief has proven to be an absolute necessity for survival. My broken heart's imagination has caused all sorts of terrestrial goings-on to show up for me. Trees, turtles, dragonflies, hawk feathers, rainbows, crickets, and eggplants have displayed a generosity of spirit. This spirituality of the natural world coming forth with visions and stories has been amazing. Living and nonliving things peeked between the cracks of the walls I'd built.

Even the rocks had a message for my broken heart. Yes, the entire created world, in grief and joy, spinning story, a spirit story.

Grief always points in the direction of what is. And it's a terrible feeling, this mournful call to a new normal, especially if simply an examination of losses. But what if something else is possible? Grief has certainly propelled me into new orbits where the rules are completely different from what I've known.

What if there's a narrative in which the love story continues? What if life can hold new tales wide enough to carry all of me, even pieces of my broken heart? What if in our grief we could shed the cloak of the mourner to become the celebrant? One whom the community regards with deep respect and love? In this imaginary world, the griever would not be pitied but given importance, a role in society as one who is in touch with some of the deepest mysteries of life. I'm curious about an imagined sacred place where the mourner is blessed and revered. In this world, all of those in community with her would be blessed as well. Here is the beginning of just such a story, a time and place on a faraway planet light-years from here:

> I chose the colors of the full moons rising over Kalima. It was a rare occurrence when sister moons show their whole faces in tandem, and rarer still when this double blessing could be viewed from the southern continent. Legend has it that two sisters, Mayon and Vaya, fell in love with the sun. Mayon, the elder sister, although she knew it was forbidden, stared directly at the sun, admiring its fiery light. She soon became enchanted by the sun's brilliance and was caught in its embrace. She whirled round and round, quite unable to break free. One day, as she passed close to her younger sister, she began to call out, "Help me, Vaya, for I am caught in this spinning torrent of brightness!" Vaya, upon hearing Mayon's call, turned to help her sister and in so doing became enchanted as well.

So together they dance, Mayon and Vaya, in orbit around the sun. And every twenty-three years they face each other in the fullness of their love for each other and the sun. It was a very good omen that we sat together upon the black sands of Kalima that one last time watching the moons rise. There were thousands gathered to witness this phenomenon and perhaps gain a measure of favor. But for us, it was as if we were the only two people in the entire first world. Our faces radiated with the blue light of Mayon and Vaya as we held our blessing stones in outstretched palms, whispering prayers for good health and fortune.

That precious moment seems to belong to another space and time. The impossible is now becoming my truth. You have died. Your spirit has been dispatched to the overworld and I am to become your celebrant. "How can this be?" I asked, shaking my head left to right again and again. No, I said silently, this is a dream, a terrible dream. Any moment now I will awaken and we will laugh together once more. You are so good, my beloved. And there's so much more to do with our beautiful lives. We had wonderful plans, did we not? To make the sacred pilgrimage to the isle of Lerat, where it is said one's purpose can be found written in the sands. To practice the inward breathing technique, opening our hearts to greater intimacy. For us to trade our dwelling (too large now that our younglings have left the nest) to live on a small boat. All of these plans are now revealing themselves to be parts of a crazy dream that is, after all, not a dream. And you, my beloved, have crossed to the overworld.

As my musings faded, something emerged that felt like a half-remembered dream. I was within the pashwan and I was to become your celebrant. But this was no dream. This was a brand-new truth. I knew what was expected, that I would be cloistered here, attended to by the elders, and initiated with the old rites and rituals. This was not required, of course; the decision to become someone's celebrant is a deeply personal one. Many souls passed to the overworld without a celebrant. They were remembered with love and honor by their families and loved ones during Shallotte, the festival of time and memory.

The pashwan was not as I'd imagined. The colors were soft, restful, like the pinky hue on the inside of a seashell. The ceilings were slung low and somehow comforting. There were no windows as such, but a circular space on the eastern wall blushed open and closed in a pattern that mimicked breathing. Lost in thought, I recalled that I'd been in the midst of choosing the colors of my tambor, the robe of remembrance. I am certain you would approve both of these colors (radiant blue-green) and of the fine workmanship of the cloth (light yet strong). Yes, these colors recall your beauty, my beloved.

"I've made my choice," I said to the woman who had been so patient while I drifted in thought. "This one is perfect." She placed the dizzying array of other fabrics, some translucent, some a heavy brocade, and still others whisper light with a luminescent quality, into the hope chest. She did not speak, knowing that I was yet untendered. She touched her right hand to the middle of her chest, bowing in the traditional gesture of respect as she left me to my peace in the semidarkness of the pashwan. I closed my eyes and the glow globes automatically adjusted their light for sleep, and I realized that I was indeed very weary. The effort it took to make this small choice of my tambor had left me exhausted.

Ah, sleep would be welcome, but would rest come? Since you crossed to the overworld, my dream life has become a wilding place, a curious country. Even in sleep I do not rest. The elders said this might be so. Sometimes they counsel me, "Sleeping may bring rest," and other times, "You will journey beyond the ridge of time." Or "It is different with every being and so we cannot say how it will be for you." In our youth we were taught that the celebrant holds space between the worlds. The cradlesong we were taught goes like this:

Light to dark to light again,
mystery unfolds, my friend.
Who holds a part holds all.
Who parts with one
Has yet lost none.
For all that lives
Lives on in all!
We fall to rise and rise to fall

With the cradlesong of my youth lulling my heart, I fell toward sleep, dimly aware of the chorus of elders encircling me. "I am honored to be your celebrant, beloved," I whispered. "As you would have been mine if I'd crossed before you." Yes, this is as it should be, our promise, our love coming full circle.

HONEY

honey...
sweet, dense, dark
calling forth
my confectionary
best self
honey...
replacing names
nick, given, borrowed.
applied like salve to sorry.
sticks and stones.
honey...
keep me lovely
in low places.
honey...
sweet drip a smoky invitation
hung on morning
clothesline
honey...
eclipsing
babysugardarlingsweetheart
not one capable
of holding its
amber gravity.
honey...
I miss your
sweet calling.

THE BOOK

I hesitate
before the paged promise.
Change has made me
a dried apple.

Thirsty.

I will open this book.
Pray that it will
lead me to cool springs.
I wish to quench the fire of loss.
Drink myself drunk, stumbling
toward possible.

I shall abandon my post
as watchkeep of the past.
This book will show me
how to rinse the clay
from underneath the fingernails
of time.

It will guide me past the danger
of yesterday's gaze.

I will then know ways
known only to those lucky few
who discovered this great book.
Who read with tender understanding
its wisdom!

My heart leaps in anticipation
as I open . . .

Every single page crisp, white
. . . waiting.

BENEATH THE SKIN OF SORROW

Awake all night, once again, running my hands through strands of darkness. Nina Simone floats past, her voice quavers, I finger my wedding band. Her fevered timbre of loss intones,

Black is the color of my true love's hair

I know that peculiar fire that burns but does not consume. She's singing something subcutaneous, something coiled beneath the skin. Sorrow, like smoke, extends an invitation to descend. It lingers at the end of each note. But I hesitate, afraid of the octave's blue depth.

I keep looking back to find the map of you.

His face, so soft and wondrous fair

Wondrous, silent, none of this is fair. I have fallen from a windy height and still . . . and still I'm falling.

The purest eyes and the strongest hands

His eyes are the night sky, blues changes, and the whole wide world shimmers inside the cup made of his golden fingers.

I love the ground on where he stands

No, I do not love it, the ruddy clay of melancholy. Prayers are standing leaves on this brave, sacred ground. Undergirding trees and roots, a mossy hymn lifts its face in generosity.

I peek beneath the floor of a world my skin believes.

Black is the color of my true love's hair
I love my lover and well he knows

"I love my lover" hums at the roof of my mouth and I tongue a confession. Fallen words sway in a downward spiral. And well he knows, sorrow song needs no text.

I love the ground on where he goes.

This holy ground requires shedding my head voice. Should I?

Naked, trembling soprano cries *Yes! Yes!* and sweeping through my sloping chest arrives on a contralto breath of praise.

And still I pray that the time will come.
When he and I will be as one

Numbers shuffle in agreement as that place opens that is neither you nor I.

Beneath the skin of sorrow, the line between us disappears.

Black is the color of my true love's hair.

LOVING-KINDNESS TEA

Ingredients

3   leaves free of distraction, each weighing at least one hour

2   quarts of gratitude

1   gallon of silence (may be punctuated by natural sounds)

3   tablespoons of I Am Enough herb (if you cannot find,
      use instead love)

1   tablespoon assorted berries of worry, shame, guilt, and regret
      crushed with mortar and pestle (fear is a good substitute for all)

Pick three leaves from the same stalk in any twenty-four-hour day. Bundle together and prepare, using the utmost care to remove all distractions. To-do lists, texts, and phone calls can be especially stubborn. Please be diligent. Place leaves in a quiet space and do not disturb while you assemble the other ingredients. Pour gratitude slowly; do not worry if you end up with more than two quarts. You may save the rest for later. It will keep and does not need to be refrigerated. Pure silence can be hard to find, but if you can manage, you will not be disappointed. Quiet will do in a pinch. Sourcing in the woods or other natural environments has often achieved good results. The herb I Am Enough is readily available but often mislabeled as vanity. Choose the brand called Just as I Am, Without One Plea. It has excellent reviews. The berries of worry etc. can be ripe or dried. They are plentiful and readily available. If you find you have none, hurray for you! Your tea will be sweeter than most. For the rest of us, crush well with mortar and pestle or food processor to a fine powder. If you skip this step, they may rise to the top, leaving an unpleasant and bitter aftertaste. Stir well. (Gratitude and love dissolve all grainy bits.) Allow to steep for a bit. Pour into a handmade cup. Garnish with mint leaves. Breathe deeply and savor your tea.

THE FIRST PAGE

You were not
the first page
of my book.
And it seems
as if
the last
page's
scribbling
is
drawn
around
your
absence.
The spine is
cracked,
bookmarked.
Open
to *that* page
going back
to before
books
or pages
or
scribbling.

I was thrilled to be chosen from the bouquet of eager hands raised, waving, pleading, "Pick me! Pick me!" in the classroom. Oh, happy day, Nnenna. The teacher deems you worthy to be the one chosen to sharpen all the pencils.

I don't know why Grief shoved me toward this interrogation of pencilhood. I hadn't actually used a pencil much since the kids were small. Pens? Yes, as they are adult instruments, which presume you'll get it right the first time. But eraser-tipped pencils naturally given to smudge and impermanence? Nope, I hadn't used them so much.

Yet there was something calling me. Something that was sounding from the perspective of the pencil itself. To get at the transformational magic of ideas, it was necessary to ditch the computer and ask the pencil directly for its story. And then without so much as a moment's notice, the following story poured out from the spirit of the pencil:

Fire in the Hole

You see, there was a fire. No one knows how it began or whether or not it could have been prevented. All I know is that one day Phil noticed what appeared to be a feeling of burning fire on his right leg. At first, it was just smoldering, but it was concerning. So, we went to the doctor, lots of doctors actually, until we found one who explained that this was a symptom of his underlying medical condition. Some medical conditions, such as multiple sclerosis, can also cause sensitivity to temperature. The doctor had seen this type of thing before and added that there was no effective treatment or cure. It would in time, he predicted, get worse. The feeling of flames reaching higher until, well . . .

We didn't want to listen anymore but had to ask, "How long before . . . you know?"

"Three to five years," the doctor said. "Maybe more, maybe less." We left the doctor's office stunned, wisps of smoke slowly rising from Phil's right shoe. Over the next weeks and months, we tried various cures that others struggling with similar "electrical fires" had suggested.

Perhaps these off-grid cures worked for some, but for us they did nothing. The fire was spreading; now it was possible to see actual flames moving up his right flank and arm. This caused a considerable challenge to Phil, who was right-handed, but in typical Phil fashion, he then taught himself to use his left. And he never complained about the flames' interference with the way he'd learned to live in his body.

This strange electrical fire that burned but did not consume (as regular fires do) became a part of his life. All too soon it became impossible for Phil to walk without assistance. But no matter whether he had to use a cane or scooter or wheelchair, Phil kept a positive attitude. He viewed these challenges as a design problem, and design problems, he said, "Always have multiple solutions."

Days, months, and years passed as the fire that had begun on his right side began to spread to his left side and beyond the borders of his body. We saw evidence of scorching in his car, his office, and certain rooms in our home. The flames made these places unsafe, so we decided, for example, that it was too risky for Phil to drive. It seemed the fire could not be contained, much less extinguished. Ordinary things one might take for granted, like cups, bowls, pens, and remote control devices, oftentimes melted. When the fire eventually reached our bed, we made a difficult decision. It was time for me to move to a cot right next to the bed we'd shared for nearly four decades.

Some nights we'd talk about our lives before the fire began, how rich and wonderful that life had been. Other times we'd discuss what might happen if the flames rose high enough to become a funeral pyre. He told me he knew that would eventually be the case.

One night in particular, in the flickering glow Phil seemed restless. I climbed into the bed with him and held him close. Heat was radiating from the mattress, sheets, blanket, pillow. I could feel it smoldering as our bodies touched.

"I'm burning up, you know," he said. "It won't be very long now."

"How do you know?" I asked, hoping that what he said wasn't true but knowing, deep down, it was.

"I know because there isn't much left of my body to burn. This fire is burning my body but not my spirit," he said.

I held him tightly, breathing the smoky air between us, knowing the truth of his words, that even fire couldn't burn fire.

This story was a literal download from my spirit pencil. Perhaps it's another truth to lay on my questing heart: Phil's fire still burns, somewhere.

A DREAM LETTER FROM PHIL

I was in a room full of letters. They were of different sizes, leaning against chairs, stacked on the floor, hanging from the ceiling, everywhere. Some were loosely arranged as words, but most were randomly scattered about. Somewhere in the distance I hear a voice, a teacher perhaps, saying, "Okay, now spell *boy*, sound it out now." B-O-Y. We were supposed to find the letters that made the word. Each letter you picked up was supposed to utter a sound, the sound associated with it.

Phil was there, and now I was an observer as he picked up letter after letter. The letters he picked up did not make the sounds one would expect. Some of them grunted and others burped or were totally silent. I could feel his frustration rising. He turned the letters this way and that, trying to figure it out.

The letter *w*, for example, mooed like a cow when held aloft, and when turned upside down uttered a soft whistle. Playing by these rules it would've been impossible to sound it out or to spell the word *boy*.

I looked away from his struggle. When I looked again, my gaze fell on a fantastic set of structures. There were beautiful buildings of various shapes and sizes. Phil had designed and constructed an entire city of buildings from those letters, and there was no concealing his sense of accomplishment and joy.

How am I to interpret this dream? For days I'd been trying to write a letter to Phil and had experienced quite a bit of inner resistance. What would really be nice, I thought, as I was stuck trying to write to him, would be to get a letter *from* Phil.

Letters, written by hand, were part of the early foundation, the sacred geometry, of our relationship. When we first met, we quickly built a bridge of spoken words. The back-and-forth written conversation was magic. Later on, living at a distance from each other, we entrusted letters with our declarations of love and desire. Our truths and their delivery were given over to strangers, uniformed men and women whose mission it was to carry such things as love letters, bills, and packages.

Was this dream vision actually a form of communication, a letter sent from Phil? A grief-attenuated opening of the veil between two worlds? Surely the rules over there must be different, no paper or pencil to be found, and no hand with which to write.

So, what then? What strategy to communicate joy and accomplishment? What shared information that only lovers know? What slice of experience and personality belonging to Phil and Phil alone? It was him and I had to write him back!

My dearest Phil,

Thank you for sending this message to my heart, so that I'd know without a doubt that it was truly you. It was perfectly composed, the room, the letters, all of it. Phil, how beautifully and artfully crafted were your buildings!

Your message was such an amazing gift, it's hard to express how much this means to me. You must know how much I miss you, and moments like this assure me that you're doing well.

I'm learning to trust in things I can't see. And you know how hard that is for a sister. You're teaching me that it's about layers, like in music. I'm digging you in the subdivisions. You are reaching for me. You, my beloved, are really pulsing beneath, around, and within the experience of what we call normal life.

I'm so happy right now for this beautiful glimpse of your living presence. Thank you, my love. I had no idea that your being gone could be so full.

I love you.

Your wife,
Nnenna

ZIP IT

I thought closing my husband's estate would bring a sense of relief, finally providing a period at the end of the sentence. It did not. At long last, I received copies of the paperwork. There were little sticky tabs indicating exactly where to sign. But instead of feeling closure, I suppressed the desire to crumple the papers and run out the door.

I felt a storm of anger and sadness, then guilt about these feelings. My beloved husband provided for our family in life and in death. The estate paperwork was evidence of that blessing and yet . . . I felt some kinda way. I would have given anything to have him in the physical form. Instead of a sense of closure, new doors swung open that I felt totally unprepared to step through. There was at this threshold new language describing Phil as the decedent and me as the surviving spouse, widow, and executrix. I was none of these. I was a Black woman beat up by life. What's the word for that? Some of the books I'd read suggested that in due time the waves of grief would abate and I'd find closure. They made it sound as if closure were something you might have just misplaced, like the TV remote. "Oh my, let me see . . . where did I put it? I just had it . . . silly me. Now where on earth could it be?" Perhaps closure could be achieved, but I wasn't convinced it was possible or even desirable.

There've been changes in my day-to-day feelings. The sharp edges of grief that were almost unbearable in the early days have given way to the more persistent throb of loss. The drone that accompanies my new normal plays on and on, coloring life in various ways. So, while I can attest to things being different after months and years have passed, I wouldn't call it closure. I continue to miss my beloved in a thousand ways, and every day reveals the subtle and bittersweet nature of that loss. Closure feels like there's a gesture of turning away—dusting off one's hands and heading in another direction. For me, that's a definite nope.

When the kids were young and Phil was at his wits' end arguing a fine point with them about what was fair—basically dadsplaining his answer, which was "No"—he'd say, "Zip it! Not another word." His tone signaled the end of the discussion. It usually worked, at least temporarily. I laughed at this memory, wishing for a magic word in my vocabulary that I could use for grief with that same kind of power.

ODE TO ZIPPER

I've long admired
your ability
to slide
smoothly into position
while announcing
It is closed.
Your sound,
particular
and significant,
is so easily
accomplished
on most days.
A toothy
glide and presto!
two
become one.
I do understand
occasionally
getting hung up,
stuck,
unable to
go any further.
Maybe having
choked
on a stray
bit of thread,

a ruff of fabric.
I, too, have
had a bit
of trouble
swallowing
recent truths.
Let us both
gently rock
back
and forth
loosening
this clench
and slide toward one.

CUFFLINKS

Cufflinks, or rather, a single cufflink. Has one ever been the cause of deep mourning and grief?

Has an encounter with an individual cufflink ever been associated with tears and heart-wrenching pain? Or have scientists studied them for possible negative effects upon the nervous systems of susceptible people?

I was simply organizing a junk drawer. My aim was to toss or give away things no longer needed or desired. Someone suggested this practice as an excellent way to clear the mind and recharge the spirit. "Objects contain energy," they said. "By mindfully choosing to let go of things you no longer need or want, you may reset your spiritual compass and make room for new energy."

This made perfect sense to me. My life had changed over the past three years. The deaths of my husband and my only sister within six months of each other created huge shifts in my day-to-day life. Grief changed my answer to the question "What's important to you now?" Sometimes a bewildered "I don't know" was all I could muster. Weighty and important things now felt rather insignificant. Uprooted by grief, every little thing felt drenched with sorrow. I longed for a spiritual refresh. And the mindful practice of clearing my home, though daunting, seemed an excellent place to start.

I imagined lifting my house from its foundation, turning it upside down, and allowing the unneeded, broken, worn-out things to spill from open doors and windows. All of the things that had *died* to me because I no longer needed or loved them would magically find themselves elsewhere. Maybe in the hands of some grateful person or in the landfill.

This was impossible, of course, and I had an inkling that the mental processes involved in tossing and sorting were tied to the subsequent healing. Nevertheless, I conjured the image of the big brown leather sofa that Phil had chosen (but that I never really liked) sliding right out the front door.

My closets were full of clothes that I'd kept mainly for sentimental reasons. I imagined them cheerily volunteering themselves for donation. The purple flowy gown I wore to the Soul Train Lady of Soul Awards; the vintage Norma Kamali pantsuit that I rocked on a photo shoot for my first feature-magazine cover; the buttery yellow number chosen by my stylist for the forty-fifth Grammy telecast with Take 6, all of these and much more would bid me a hearty and fond farewell.

"Yeah, sister, we don't fit you anymore," they'd whisper. "But we sure had fun, didn't we?"

"Yes," I'd agree, smiling, while silently waving goodbye as they floated off to new adventures.

To tell the truth, I was weary of standing before my closet with an apology for my body that no longer fit into these clothes and memories. I wasn't willing to offer promises of weekly crunches to find the waistline I had ten years ago. To make solemn vows that one day, I would wear these outfits again, thereby recapturing the good old days, seemed both ridiculous and exhausting. I scanned my body, my now-body, offering thanks that it is well and strong. It holds a certain softness around the breasts, belly, and thighs. Hips that I'd dreamed of when I was younger can now be found in the mirror. Crinkles dance 'round corners of my eyes, and when I smile, tiny lines giggle in appreciation of love and joy. And these silvery strands on my head? I'm grateful for them showing up at all when they could have chosen not to.

Sure, I knew this flight of fancy was a form of procrastination, but hopefully in a good way. Maybe I was simultaneously readying my heart for the mission at hand. This soul sorting and tossing was a big job, yet I was determined to make way for beautiful new energies. In looking around for a good place to start, I considered my bedroom but felt it might be too much to tackle first. The closets, bathrooms, office, and living room were also under consideration, and each of them held their own challenges. It was then that I remembered the advice to begin small to avoid discouraging oneself. "Choose a task," it was suggested, "that you might accomplish in a couple hours, like a junk drawer."

Now that sounded perfect! I had several junk drawers, at least one, it seemed, in every room. I chose a drawer in my laundry room where, I reasoned, there'd be a high probability of success. Surely, the laundry room junk drawer must rank pretty low on the Richter scale. I was already celebrating having accomplished one step on the road to my spiritual reset. What joy! in tossing half-empty bottles of stain remover, laundry starch, iron-on patches, a broken seam ripper, and old, scentless lavender sachets. And what freedom! in donating travel-size soaps, shampoos, and conditioners, wool dryer balls, lint rollers, mesh lingerie bags, odd buttons, needles and thread, safety pins, bobby pins, and coins expelled from pockets during the wash. I was here for it. All of it.

I quickly grabbed two bags, one bound for trash and one for Goodwill. Opening the drawer, I discovered some of the aforementioned items, but there was a far greater variety of stuff than I'd anticipated. Laundry adjacent? Yes. And then decidedly not-laundry bits, like a broken device that I recognized but whose function I couldn't name. Several flashlights, all dead. Old batteries, scissors, essential oil bottles, twine, wine corks for an unfinished art project, my granddaughter's pink and purple barrettes, dried-up glue sticks, broken eyeglasses, old remote controls, fossilized chewing gum, expired antibiotics and other medications, shoehorn, assorted pencils, pens, an empty Vaseline container, old toothbrushes used for cleaning, and finally, a lone cufflink.

It was gold, inset with an oval stone burnished orange, carnelian maybe? It wasn't one of Phil's favorites, but he wore the pair often enough. I held it in my hand. Felt its weight. It was heavy for its size. A feeling I couldn't quite describe ushered a flashback of Phil dressed in a crisp white shirt with French cuffs. "Good looking, looking good," I used to say to him.

Phil took great pride in his appearance, not a hair out of place nor a stray piece of lint. His custom-tailored shirts were part of a total package. It didn't matter that a shirtsleeve was barely visible once he donned a sport coat or suit jacket. The cufflink made its point every time he raised his long arms. Holding the cufflink and the memories, I wondered where the other one could be. I pushed aside my earlier goals of spiritual cleansing, thinking, "It must be in here somewhere."

I tossed things about, emptying the drawer, needing to find the other cufflink. It was the mate to the one now warm in my hand, but it wasn't there. The drawer, now empty, had held just one cufflink. I cried at the ridiculous notion of a single cufflink and for all the unmatched pairs lost in the bottoms of drawers, for myself in the midst of a search for spiritual refreshment in my laundry room, for everything I couldn't name. I wept for all of it.

After a while, I sat staring at the cufflink, trying to decide whether to continue searching for the other one. Then at least, I reasoned, I could give both of them to one of my sons. But something told me looking for it would be a waste of time, and that I'd missed the point entirely.

This single cufflink was simply a sweet gift from Phil.

THE BAG

I brought
my imagination
to the mourning
bench.
I had to.
There was
so little time.
She said to bring
something you
value.
And be quick
about it.
Without context,
or knowing what
would be best,
I grabbed
what I could reach
and hurried
to meet
my
particular grief.
What's in the bag?
she asked.
Imagination,
I said,
certain

the ghosts
lingering
by her side
would laugh.
Nice choice,
she said.
Now let us
begin.

RECURRING DREAM

The same dream again tonight.
I'm driving,
shifting into fifth gear
with my eyes closed.
I try, but cannot open them.
The road lies
half remembered
before me.
I can't see. I can't see . . .
speeding past post and beam,
praying I don't crash.
Perhaps it's actually you
driving.
Your slender fingers
sheltering mine.
You whisper
"It's obvious—
what you cannot see
needs
no seeing."

YOUR ASHES

The lake looks different
to me now.
It seems to have thickened
as if it's become
more precious,
viscous.
The turtles wait in line
as they do
every morning
to enjoy the
sun-warmed tree.
The one submerged
by the storm
winters ago.
Grace that the lake
and tree
agreed to hold
each other
for a while.
The hawk draws
lazy circles
above my head.
Her vision is
sharper than
mine.
Perhaps she's

gathering
evidence that
you are there.
Last night,
the geese
ruffled my sleep
and I swear
I could hear
you
laughing with them.

Every New Year's Day, the same ritual. Phil pulled out his journal, insisting that we write down individual and collective one-year, five-year, and ten-year goals. Early in our marriage, with the care of three little ones in my orbit, I thought this practice was a bit silly. I mean, getting to the point where all the kids were consistently using the potty seemed like a less than lofty reach. At that time, my list for year one always revolved around getting more sleep and being organized, and when I tried to think of goals for a period five and ten years in the future, I might as well have been asked to write a fairy tale. My very short list was composed of things that felt quite impossible. Phil's list always seemed to be specific and filled with audacious purpose. It was clear that he believed his goals achievable. When I bemoaned my lack of imaginative clarity, he said, "Don't worry so much about how it'll happen, just write your dreams on paper." Over the years, I learned to trust the universe. My goal-setting became more intentional. It's not as if everything came true in ways I'd imagined, but I noticed what was activated in the realm of everyday life little by little assuming a dreamt-of shape.

Another year is on the horizon. I sit alone, readying my heart to write. I wish for a stiff breeze that overwhelms the idea of a permanent, immutable sorrow. *Don't worry so much about how it'll happen, just write* swims into my head once again.

I want to recognize joy upon arrival, even when it's on tiptoe. I want to notice it, to be warmed by its incandescence. I'd like the clay of every day to be soft enough to work with my bare hands and strong enough to hold a pleasing shape. I want to write what could be an unsingable melody across the wide octave of the grim and glorious. I want to take my unsubmerged losses, fashion them into bright beads, string them in the light of the present, and wear this rosary of love and hope.

AFTER TIME

We will watch with our hearts instead.
After time, spring will be just what happens when
daffodils raise their heads in yellow laughter
and bluebirds, gossiping, return.
After time, we will gather all the wasted and the lost. We will build
    fires and melt them down
to thick, sweet syrup.
After time, it will be difficult to call your arrival
expected, early, or late.
We will be happy, surprised, or annoyed
and that is all.
After time, yesterday will be unthinkable, and tomorrow,
    a fairy tale.
After time, I will no longer scratch
memory's face
for something
too small
to be
you.

REMEMBER YOU

"I Remember You" is the name of an old standard with a Johnny Mercer lyric. It's a song I've sung onstage on many occasions, and now it feels like a soul activity I engage in every day.

I'm learning to be open to receiving you daily, hourly, and sometimes moment to moment. And every time, upon your arrival it feels like a re-creation. Memories play a part, but memory alone is remarkably unreliable. Sometimes they're out of it at the corner market. I've heard that more than once lately: "It's on back order; supply chain issues, you know."

Besides, sensing you in exquisite detail as often as I do requires sturdier materials than memory affords. The past is written on flimsy paper. And if you use the same paper a lot, it begins to degrade, rip, and tear. The time-smudged pages become quite worn, and after a while, well, they just make you feel some kinda long-ago-and-faraway sad.

To remember you is to accept you again and again within the puzzle of my life, to experience you afresh in new, interesting, and pleasurable ways. I reach for and find you in the call-and-response of the everyday. It's exciting to notice the ways in which you show up as unmistakably yourself—in the now.

Yes, beloved, you are my new discovery. A region of previously uncharted space. I will boldly go with a lover's imagination. Your intricate patterns, no longer encased in solid form, are expansive, universal, and real. You are the gathering dream, a vast living world—and curious, I cannot resist. I am at once conjurer and explorer eager for you and those sensations turning at the rim of the unknowable. You are the open door to flowering visions, new formations, right here, right now.

I remember you.

ASK THE OLD WOMAN

The one who lives behind the garden gate.
The one whose yard is
full of outrageous.
Ask the old woman who lives alone
yet is not lonely.
Ask her if the silver chords in her hair play the blues
or speak in tongues.
Ask the woman,
the old one,
the one who taught her children to swallow the moon
and watched as they walked out the door
and returned full, spitting seeds.
Ask her.
Ask what she's stirring in that pot that smells so good
and why her cat who has but one eye and is blind in the other
keeps staring at you.
Ask the woman about the herbs drying in her kitchen.
Ask her which one eases labor
and which one brings the wayward lover to your doorstep.
Ask her the meaning of the words on her medicine jars
compassion, joy, forgiveness, gratitude ... patience.
Why is the one marked "patience" the biggest of all?
Ask her.
Ask the old woman why she covers all the mirrors with her scarves
and fasts for 21 days
when a spirit departs.

Ask why she walks backward from the altar.
Ask her about the blood
in the small bowl on the high shelf.
Ask her, ask her! about her lovers . . .
and ask why her smile broadens at the mention of her name.
Ask her where she keeps her measuring tape, hourglass,
    and yardstick.
Ask why the clocks have faces but no hands.
Ask the old woman who smells of sassafras, sage, and ashes.
Ask the old one.
Ask her
what she keeps in that box beneath her bed.
Ask her for the name of the song she
keeps humming.
Ask the old woman. . . . Ask her.

YOU'LL KNOW

That Grief is through with you
when her trembling hands
unclench the breath
you've been holding
since then.
And beauty,
for so long in rehearsal,
knows her lines,
sashays to center
calling *come closer!*
You'll know by the smell
of smoke.
Her fires,
having consumed
all combustible light,
cast glowing
soul embers,
smelted forms
of what was.
You'll know
when the sprawling
solitude sings a
rustling of invitation.
When Grief is through
with *this* part
of you, you'll know.

Coda

GRATITUDE

Thank you, beloved grief sojourner.

When my mother was really pleased, she'd say, "You got my joy bells ringing." I love the idea of joy as a bell. I imagine being that bell, my brown burnished shoulders stretching across the sky, delighting in advance of the struck sound. The clapper, in no real hurry, pays attention to the angle of swing and its inevitable journey. The rim ripples with anticipation, vibrates with laughter as the iron air in my wide mouth unclasps on the exhale—*ding! dong!*

Of course, the wild, dissonant bells of sorrow swing back and forth too, ringing in ordinary days collapsed by absence. The singer in my soul wants to *make* something out of having been struck—to improvise amid the bells tolling *gone, gone, gone.* My losses led me to embark on a pilgrimage, and daily, I'm still on that road to be coming.

Your grief is yours alone—unique in its belonging, longing, and expression. We're all cast in grief's twilight, unable to control or contain it, and we're bathed in its constant glow. The corners of your life may be occupied by shadows, and you may think that this will always be. But trust, there is a bone-deep wisdom growing in and around your life.

The idea that *grief changes you* is well known, but the thought that *you may transform your grief* isn't as often explored. Improvising with grief is a continuous dance, as you (and grief) birth and re-birth new versions of your now known universe. I searched for a definition of *inflammation*, which read, "A normal part of the body's response to injury or infection," and it struck me that grief is like an inflammation of the spirit. The word *normal* almost leapt off the page. I hope that an improvisational response to our grief can become just that—normal.

It might be difficult to understand right now as you're reading these words, but you are actually growing alongside your grief. Even though it may feel as if nothing is moving except your trembling heart.

Sorrow makes us permeable, subject to the world in new and often uncomfortable ways. In whatever ways that hold meaning for you, ask yourself, "What else is possible?" The tender spaces exposed by our losses might be ready for gentle exploration. As strange as it may sound, by reclaiming my creative practice within grief, I've gained a sense of agency and comfort. Every day I'm discovering what else lies within the folds of sorrow's long and heavily embroidered gown. Writing and singing is helping me on my journey to a life I want to fall in love with again.

In the jazz world, when one uses the phrase "You dig?" it refers to an inquiry about deep understanding. "Can you dig it?" is a query about the subtle, complicated, and often hidden nature of a thing. Digging in creative dialogue with loss and learning to improvise on the changes in and around my life story have allowed me to nod my head in agreement—at least a little bit—and for this, I am grateful.

I'm not fully there; on some days I'm full of argument about this or that situation.

But one day, I dream of taking the entire world in my arms and singing, "I love you, my one wild, chaotic, and precious life! And my wish is that this bright moment be yours as well."

CADENZA

The calendar tells us a story, and in the end that's all it really is. It's a story attempting to explain the mystery of our lived human experience. "How long has it been?" is a question, a bell really, that continues to ring in my soul as I mourn my beloved husband Phil, my sister Debbie, and my best dog Basie.

Now the question becomes, "What do I seek as I travel back to that July morning in 2019 or the January afternoon in 2020 when the stars collided and suddenly winked off?" Am I checking to see if it's been long enough? It is time for my gaze to turn away from the past and "move on"? I'm learning that while the calendar may hold some everyday wisdom where grief is concerned, it's not the most useful or satisfying tool. There is no set day or month to move on, and there's no time limit on grief.

Some say, "You have to be strong." Others suggest, "You need closure." I've also been told that it "gets better" with time. But I've looked at the calendar and counted the days, and here's what my grief experience has taught and continues to teach me: Being strong is difficult to sustain, and it's not the best use of what's often a limited supply of energy. I'm learning to accept bits of grace offered from my family, the hearts of friends, and strangers, from my art practice, and from the abundant natural world. I'm discovering that rather than summoning superwoman strength to withstand the pain, the well of creativity and imagination can sustain and guide me on this grief journey.

And yet, I still must say *Yes* to my tears, anger, fear, and heartache. *Yes* to No. *Yes* to the sometimes unbearable quiet. *Yes* to the damnable and particular situations when missing him means staying in bed all day. *Yes* to curiosity. *Yes* to intimate dialogue with Grief herself, because at times she needs a good talking-to. *Yes* to beauty inviting me to come closer. *Yes* to setting boundaries. *Yes* to dark chocolate and other pleasures. *Yes* to writing my story as it unfolds. *Yes* to midday naps (because grieving is a full-time job). *Yes* to changing my mind as often as I choose. *Yes* to singing new songs. *Yes* to forgiving life one day at a time. *Yes* to refusing to care one whit about the Department of They. *Yes* to it all.

For me, grief is not at all about closure. It's about learning to be widespread in this crazy life, open in ways I didn't think possible. Our nearly forty years of love opened doors through which rivers of goodness flow: children, grandchildren, friends, careers, artful beingness—all of that.

Does it get better? Well, so far, I can tell you, it does get *different*, and certain moments definitely feel better. It's harder to find those better ones when they're mixed within the mourning bowl, but they are there. Every day I try to reach for at least one joy-suffused moment, one deep breath untangled by the haze of sorrow. And sometimes, well, that's all a sister needs to make it on through.

With deep gratitude,
Nnenna Freelon

ACKNOWLEDGMENTS

I didn't intend to write a book about my grief. As the old Rodgers and Hart song goes, it never entered my mind. Yet, within the hub of wild darkness when sleep was wafer thin, I discovered song and story quietly marching in lockstep with this new unasked-for life. And so, I must give thanks for the chambers of solitude that birthed this book.

I'm so grateful to jazz mentors on both sides of the veil: Ellis Marsalis, Dr. Yusef Lateef, Keter Betts, Larry Reni Thomas, Geri Allen, Charles Ellison, Marian McPartland, Norman Simmons, Barry Harris, Brother Yusuf Salim, Donald Meade, Sheila Jordan, Dr. Billy Taylor, and many others. So often, I encountered improvisational lessons riding on the edge of grief's low rumble. And you were there, summoning. "Sing the octave." "Play with the silence." "Change the key." Thank you for the borrowed breath I never knew would be needed.

Lindsay Foster Thomas, Stacia Brown, Sean Roux, Cierra Brown Hinton, and Alysia Nicole Harris, thank you for your believing that my stories could be medicine.

Thank you, Andrew Berinson, for your willingness to play so beautifully in uncharted waters. Thank you, OnlyUs Media, Rowdy, and Rem, for the love and partnership.

As these stories coalesced and shape-shifted into a book, Lois Deloatch, it was your enthusiasm and gentle correction that helped me to realize this dream. Julianne Jagour and Nick Phillips, thanks for your keen eye and perspective.

To my beautiful children, Deen, Maya, and Pierce; to Kate, Jess, and Katye and my lovely grands: I love you to the moon and back. Thank you, Aunt Betty—you helped me to *know* the way. To Dr. Karla Holloway, deep gratitude for love and connection. To my agents Erika Stevens and Charlotte Sheedy, thank you for your tireless efforts and belief in this book. To Ken Wissoker and the team at Duke University Press, I'm so grateful to be working together after all these years. Thank you, EKA and Ed Keane, for your continued support.

My daughter Maya Freelon's artwork graces the cover of this book. Her color-drenched tissue paper monoprint is a combination of fragility and strength. I marvel at her visual expression of the unpredictable nature of grief. Beloved daughter, these are hard rhythms. I'm grateful to share this journey with you.

Lyrics in "Widow Song," "Just You," and "These Stories We Hold" are reprinted with the permission of Chimusic Co./ASCAP.

Nnenna Freelon, seven-time Grammy-nominated jazz singer, song-writer, storyteller, and self-proclaimed improvisational human, has enjoyed a storied career spanning over four decades. She's toured internationally, appeared on television and in films, and received numerous accolades and awards, including induction into the North Carolina Music Hall of Fame.

The 2019 death of her husband Phil Freelon, renowned architect of record of the Smithsonian Museum of African American History and Culture, from ALS, followed by the death of her sister six months later, introduced her to what she calls a *great grief*. Her award-winning podcast of the same name is an exploration of these and other losses. Between what she's lost and found, her writing is a tether.

Freelon lives in North Carolina close to her three children, Deen, Maya, and Pierce Freelon, seven grandchildren, and two dogs.

www.nnenna.com